MANAGING ANGE

Mary Hartley, the author of *T
was born in London and lives in Guildford. She divides her
time between writing books and articles and leading courses
and workshops in aspects of personal development.

Overcoming Common Problems Series

For a full list of titles please contact
Sheldon Press, 1 Marylebone Road, London NW1 4DU

Antioxidants
Dr Robert Youngson

The Assertiveness Workbook
Joanna Gutmann

Beating the Comfort Trap
Dr Windy Dryden and Jack Gordon

Body Language
Allan Pease

Body Language in Relationships
David Cohen

Calm Down
Dr Paul Hauck

Cancer – A Family Affair
Neville Shone

The Cancer Guide for Men
Helen Beare and Neil Priddy

The Candida Diet Book
Karen Brody

Caring for Your Elderly Parent
Julia Burton-Jones

Cider Vinegar
Margaret Hills

Comfort for Depression
Janet Horwood

Considering Adoption?
Sarah Biggs

Coping Successfully with Hay Fever
Dr Robert Youngson

Coping Successfully with Pain
Neville Shone

Coping Successfully with Panic Attacks
Shirley Trickett

Coping Successfully with PMS
Karen Evennett

Coping Successfully with Prostate Problems
Rosy Reynolds

Coping Successfully with RSI
Maggie Black and Penny Gray

Coping Successfully with Your Hiatus Hernia
Dr Tom Smith

Coping Successfully with Your Irritable Bladder
Dr Jennifer Hunt

Coping Successfully with Your Irritable Bowel
Rosemary Nicol

Coping When Your Child Has Special Needs
Suzanne Askham

Coping with Anxiety and Depression
Shirley Trickett

Coping with Blushing
Dr Robert Edelmann

Coping with Bronchitis and Emphysema
Dr Tom Smith

Coping with Candida
Shirley Trickett

Coping with Chronic Fatigue
Trudie Chalder

Coping with Coeliac Disease
Karen Brody

Coping with Cystitis
Caroline Clayton

Coping with Depression and Elation
Dr Patrick McKeon

Coping with Eczema
Dr Robert Youngson

Coping with Endometriosis
Jo Mears

Coping with Epilepsy
Fiona Marshall and
Dr Pamela Crawford

Coping with Fibroids
Mary-Claire Mason

Coping with Gallstones
Dr Joan Gomez

Coping with Headaches and Migraine
Shirley Trickett

Coping with a Hernia
Dr David Delvin

Coping with Long-Term Illness
Barbara Baker

Coping with the Menopause
Janet Horwood

Coping with Psoriasis
Professor Ronald Marks

Coping with Rheumatism and Arthritis
Dr Robert Youngson

Overcoming Common Problems Series

Overcoming Common Problems Series

650·1 HART

Overcoming Common Problems

Managing Anger at Work

Mary Hartley

sheldon PRESS

i 14454889

Published in Great Britain in 2002 by
Sheldon Press
1 Marylebone Road
London NW1 4DU

© Mary Hartley 2002

All rights reserved. No part of this book may be reproduced
or transmitted in any form or by any means, electronic or
mechanical, including photocopying, recording, or by any
information storage and retrieval system, without
permission in writing from the publisher.

British Library Cataloguing-in-Publication Data
A catalogue record for this book is available from
the British Library

ISBN 0-85969-856-4

Typeset by Deltatype Limited, Birkenhead, Merseyside
Printed in Great Britain by Biddles Ltd
www.biddles.co.uk

Contents

1

The Roots of Anger

What is anger?

Anger is a complex emotion, made up of different reactions which range from feelings of mild irritation to extreme fury. We all feel anger to some extent at some points in our lives, and may well associate this feeling with uncomfortable experiences of loss, frustration, helplessness, threat. Our own anger can scare us, and other people's expressions of hostility can be frightening and intimidating. We have become familiar with stories about 'road rage' and 'air rage' where anger becomes so out of control that it leads to violence and puts lives in danger. Accounts of 'desk rage' and 'photocopier rage' have not hit the headlines as yet, but a recent survey of 4,200 British workers revealed that one worker in four regularly kicked their computer or lashed out at their monitors in angry response to such things as an overload of emails or a series of computer glitches and errors. This kind of anger and frustration can result in verbal or physical attacks directed not just at objects but at other people as well. The British Crime Survey published in 2001 reported 1.2 million incidents of work-related violence. Uncontrolled expressions of anger harm everyone – the angry person, the other people involved and the organization itself. Although there is a difference between anger and rage, in that anger is not always passionate and furious, anger can be just as harmful as rage in its immediate and long-term effects. Unresolved anger and conflict at work can cause high levels of dissatisfaction, leading to low morale, poor productivity and destructive relationships.

How anger works

Anger is the feeling of displeasure that we experience when we feel threatened or frustrated. It is the emotional reaction we experience when we perceive that our needs are not being met. Anger is a natural response that we experience physically and emotionally, and also through our thoughts and behaviour. All areas of human functioning – our physical responses, our thoughts, our feelings, and our behaviour – come into play when an anger response is triggered. We respond physically to the stimulus, exhibiting the bodily changes which accompany the tension that is generated when we are faced

ACTIVITY 1: An anger quiz

Find out what you already know about anger and how it works. Tick each statement according to whether you think it is true or false. If you like, you could add to the list some of your own ideas about anger.

	True	*False*
1 Any anxiety-producing situation can lead to anger.	☐	☐
2 Feeling angry is something you grow out of.	☐	☐
3 Anger can control your thoughts.	☐	☐
4 Anger can help to release tension in a constructive way.	☐	☐
5 Anger is an emotion.	☐	☐
6 Anger is the same as aggression.	☐	☐
7 Anger is not a behaviour.	☐	☐
8 It is not normal to feel angry.	☐	☐
9 Anger will go away if you ignore it.	☐	☐
10 Not getting angry means letting someone get away with something.	☐	☐

Your ideas:

11 _____   ☐   ☐

12 _____   ☐   ☐

You will find the answers at the end of the chapter.

---

with a threat. Then we develop angry thoughts and feelings, which influence how we behave. Although the process is the same for everyone, we all respond differently according to our individual make-up. An event that **triggers** your anger may be just a mild, fleeting irritation for someone else – or may not even be noticed! Your physical response when you feel angry is automatic, indicating your body's preparation to deal with the threat, but it will not be identical to someone else's physical reaction because the nature and the intensity of your response depend on your own perception of the threat. Other factors such as your state of physical and emotional health at the time also influence your body's response to anger. The emotions that accompany the physical response are linked to your own ideas about yourself and other people, and to your personal values. The thought processes you go through – probably without realizing that you are doing so – reflect your emotional response, and lead to particular kinds of behaviour. The way that you behave when you are angry may be very different from the way your colleague behaves.

Once your anger is triggered, unless something happens to defuse the situation and calm you down, your angry feelings **escalate** as you become more aroused and move towards boiling or **crisis** point. This is the stage at which your anger might increase until it erupts in a violent outburst. After this, your angry feelings begin to **subside** and you move into a calmer mode as your body returns to normal – unless the anger response is triggered again. It can take about one and a half hours for your body to return to normal after such an angry explosion. The final stage in the process is the emotional and physical **aftermath** of angry behaviour as your body and mind recover from the high state of arousal. You are left feeling drained and depressed, and possibly guilty about what has happened.

The more angry you become, the less you are able to think, speak or listen rationally. When your anger is at boiling point you are unable to take in what is being said to you, and your judgement of events is distorted and irrational. As you calm down, you begin to think more clearly, and you are able to listen to others.

If you have frequent violent explosions of anger, this is the cycle that you will experience over and over again. It is harmful to your mental and physical health – too much anger is dangerous and can be fatal, as we'll see in Chapter 2.

> The angrier you get and stay, the more likely you are to die young.
> *Ron Potter-Efron, psychotherapist*

Scene 1: Damian's private email

The following example illustrates the sequence of events that occur when the anger response is triggered.

Lynn looks up from her work and glances over at Damian's screen. Damian is working on a personal project – again – although he knows that she is waiting for the report that he is meant to be completing for her. Her shoulders become tense and she is aware of a wave of irritation sweeping over her. Damian should not be using office time like that, particularly if it means that the project will be held up. She has promised that all the work will be completed by the end of the day. She longs to say something to Damian, but is concerned that if she does speak to him about it, her voice will shake and she will look silly. Worse than that, she might lose her temper. Lynn tries to concentrate on what she is doing, but is too wound up to get much done. When Oliver asks her something, her reply is short and snappy.

Lynn's anger is triggered by the sight of Damian working on a personal project. The anger affects her physically and emotionally, and her angry thoughts about Damian's behaviour affect her own behaviour. If Lynn does not manage her angry feelings in a different way, it is possible that they will become more intense and more difficult to control.

You may be surprised that the responsibility for the situation lies with Lynn. After all, you may be thinking, Damian is in the wrong. However, whether Damian is in the wrong or not, it is not his behaviour that causes Lynn to be angry. It is Lynn's response to his behaviour that causes her to be angry, and her response is shaped by factors such as her perception of Damian and her own approach to work. Lynn's own thoughts create her anger, and she can choose how to deal with her thoughts and how to manage her behaviour. Acquiring a good understanding of the thought patterns that make us angry and the actions they lead to, and learning how to change those thoughts and actions are key steps in managing anger.

Managing anger effectively means committing yourself to developing new patterns of thought and behaviour. It means taking responsibility for yourself rather than blaming other people and external situations.

What is wrong with being angry?

In the right circumstances, there is nothing wrong with anger. Anger is an essential tool for survival. We are programmed to feel anger so that we can deal with threats to our well-being. The physical characteristics of this powerful emotion are designed to enable us to deal with danger, sending signals that our bodies and minds are being roused to take action. The anger response is natural and necessary. There is nothing wrong with healthy anger, that is, anger which is based on sound beliefs and is expressed appropriately. But many of us need to learn how to manage anger in this way – it isn't automatic.

> Anyone can become angry – that is easy, but to be angry with the right person, to the right degree, at the right time, for the right purpose, and in the right way – this is not easy.
>
> *Aristotle*

Managing anger effectively is certainly not easy, but it is essential for a healthy life. When anger is suppressed or when it is released in a destructive way it can lead to a range of physical and mental disorders. It can prevent us from being happy and fulfilled in our personal and professional lives. We can become caught in a chain of negative thoughts in which our anger arousal constantly leads to behaviour which is destructive to ourselves and to others.

Every workplace has its share of conflict. Different personalities, heavy workloads, the pressure of deadlines and all the other demands of the work environment create tension and frustration. There is nothing wrong with this situation – it is normal and inevitable. However, it becomes destructive if negative feelings are not dealt with appropriately. A situation where hostility seethes under the surface, or where there are constant angry explosions, is unhealthy and unproductive. You may be familiar with people whose anger has affected their working life. It may be a manager whose outbursts of angry speech and behaviour causes loss of morale and productivity, or a team member who is habitually disgruntled and unmotivated, moving from position to position or job to job, resentful of others who manage their emotions and behaviour at work more positively.

Some of the consequences of not managing your behaviour at work are:

- You lose credibility.
- Your self-esteem is damaged.
- You are seen as unprofessional.

Anger is a sign that something is wrong. It alerts us to the presence of a threat or a problem. But anger does not solve the problem.

ACTIVITY 2: Managing anger

What are the benefits to you of learning to manage your own and other people's anger? Fill in the chart below.

What I will gain from managing anger effectively

1 _____

2 _____

3 _____

4 _____

What might be the consequences to me
of not managing anger effectively?

1 _____

2 _____

3 _____

4 _____

Why we get angry

Anger does not come from the event, it comes from our minds. We feel angry because we are hurt, and we are hurt because we perceive that something important to us is being threatened. We might feel threatened physically, or emotionally, or even financially. There are three areas in which most of us feel vulnerable: our self-esteem, ourselves and our property, and the needs which motivate us. When any one of these aspects is under attack, or perceived to be, our anger is triggered. Think about Lynn in Scene 1. It is likely that, as she sees it, Damian's behaviour is damaging to her self-esteem and to her ability to get her needs met. It is important to Lynn to be seen as an efficient worker who keeps to deadlines. She needs to be respected, and wants to achieve what she sets out to do. Damian's behaviour is frustrating her needs. It is likely that someone who is driven by different needs would see his behaviour differently.

Take some time now to explore your own sense of yourself and your own needs. The more self-aware you are, the more you will be able to manage your thoughts and behaviour. Once you are aware of aspects of your personality that may contribute to angry feelings, you are in a position to understand your responses, and to move on to make any changes in the way you think and behave.

The need for self-esteem

We sometimes respond angrily when we feel that our view of ourselves is being damaged by someone's behaviour. Anger is provoked when we perceive that our self-esteem or feeling of self-worth is threatened. This is particularly likely to happen if your self-esteem is based on what you see as others' assessment of you or on their behaviour towards you. When critical comments annoy you, or when you are angry because you feel that you are being made fun of, or excluded from something, you are responding to a threat to your self-esteem. How do you see yourself? What conditions are necessary for you to have a strong sense of self-worth? Your self-esteem could be linked to the amount of money that you earn, or it may depend on being respected by other people.

The need to protect ourselves and our possessions

We respond strongly when we feel that our personal comfort and safety are being threatened. When our feeling of personal security is under attack, we can experience a number of responses, one of which is anger. At work, this feeling can be aroused by all kinds of events. You might become angry when you feel that your position at work is at risk, or you might have a very strong territorial instinct and find yourself getting annoyed when people invade your space or when they help themselves to personal items such as your pen or stapler. Someone else using your desk or work area, or even colleagues eating into your time by stopping to chat can trigger your anger. Often, insecurity brings with it some degree of fear, and as you will see in Chapter 2, the physiological reactions of fear and anger are virtually identical.

ACTIVITY 3: Self-esteem

(a) Complete the following sentence as many times as you wish.
In order to think well of myself, it is necessary that . . .
(b) Think of three occasions when your self-esteem was threatened by something that happened at work.

	Event	*How I felt*	*What I did*
1			
2			
3			

Scene 2: Working late again

Stuart watches out of the corner of his eye as Geraldine crosses the floor towards him. He knows that she is going to ask him to work late again. He had planned to go to the gym straight after work and then cook his special pasta dish for himself and Sara. It will take him at least an hour and a half to input the new data, and his evening will be ruined. He fumes under his breath as Geraldine approaches, her face fixed in the smile she always uses when she wants to get someone to do something. He would like to wipe the smile off her face.

Here, Stuart's sense of well-being is threatened by the situation. His plans for the evening are important to him, and his personal comfort is being violated by Geraldine's behaviour.

Your motivating needs

Your behaviour at work is geared towards reaching goals that satisfy your needs. Angry feelings at work often arise when people are prevented from reaching their goals and feel that their needs are thwarted. Their anger is a result of frustration at not having their needs met.

ACTIVITY 4: Comfort and security

(a) What are your feelings about your personal comfort and security? What are your feelings about your property?
Complete the following sentence as many times as you wish.
I feel that my person and my property are being threatened when . . .
(b) Think of three occasions when you felt that an occurrence at work was a threat to your feeling of security.

Event	*How I felt*	*What I did*
1		
2		
3		

Scene 3: Bina's isolation

Sue notices that Bina's work has become careless. When she draws attention to her mistakes Bina responds in an offhand way that Sue finds rude. Sue doesn't understand why this is happening – Bina has been put in charge of this project because of her competence and ability, and she has been given an office of her own and a salary bonus. Why is she behaving in this way? Sue feels baffled, and is becoming increasingly annoyed with Bina.

What Sue does not realize is that Bina also is angry and frustrated. Bina enjoyed working in the laboratory with the others, and looked forward to the daily gossip and chat. Now she is isolated in her new office, and the rise in status and financial payment do not compensate for the loss of social interaction.

ACTIVITY 5: What motivates you?

Think about the kinds of needs that motivate you at work, and decide how important each one is. Use the list below to help you to focus on what is important to you, and on a scale of 1 to 9 (9 being the highest) ring the number that corresponds to the strength of each need. You could add your own examples to the list.

The need for stability and security   1 2 3 4 5 6 7 8 9

The need for change and variety   1 2 3 4 5 6 7 8 9

The need for money   1 2 3 4 5 6 7 8 9

The need to achieve   1 2 3 4 5 6 7 8 9

The need to be appreciated   1 2 3 4 5 6 7 8 9

The need to be challenged   1 2 3 4 5 6 7 8 9

The need for social interaction   1 2 3 4 5 6 7 8 9

The need for status   1 2 3 4 5 6 7 8 9

The need for power and influence   1 2 3 4 5 6 7 8 9

The need to be creative   1 2 3 4 5 6 7 8 9

The need to be liked   1 2 3 4 5 6 7 8 9

Your ideas:

_____   1 2 3 4 5 6 7 8 9

_____   1 2 3 4 5 6 7 8 9

What lies behind angry feelings?

Of course, the angry emotions experienced by the people in the previous scenes could be based on well-founded perceptions, and the feelings could be dealt with healthily and productively. But as we know, this is not always the case. The kind of unwelcome, destructive anger that leads to unpleasant situations is often based on unhelpful ways of thinking. You may have certain patterns of thought and certain assumptions that cause you to be angry. These thoughts may be illogical and unrealistic, based on nothing other than your own ideas about the world (which may not be helpful or realistic) and your own interpretation of situations and the behaviour of others (which may be distorted and inaccurate). Your angry responses may be triggered by particular habits of thinking. Without realizing it, your ingrained beliefs and attitudes could be making you vulnerable to threat, causing you to react angrily when you perceive that your values are being challenged, or that your negative assumptions and expectations are being confirmed. You may recognize aspects of your own or others' thought patterns in the following examples of typical patterns of thinking that can contribute to anger.

The end of the world
Remember Lynn from Scene 1? At the end of the working day, she is still angry. She meets a friend for a drink, and tells her about Damian's behaviour.

'It makes me so angry!' she exclaims. 'It's the way he just pleases himself and uses the firm's time for his own purposes. I think it's appalling. If everyone had his attitude we wouldn't get any work done and we'd end up losing all our major accounts.'

Jane sighs. Lynn exaggerates so much, making everything a hundred times worse than it really was. It is quite entertaining sometimes, listening to her rants, but it does become a bit wearing, and getting worked up like that doesn't do Lynn any good.

'Come on,' she says. 'I know it's annoying, but it's not that bad. And it's hardly likely that you will lose all your business because of Damian doing some personal emails!'

But Lynn isn't prepared to listen to another point of view. 'It's all right for you, you don't have to deal with him every day. You've no idea how awful it is!'

The tendency to exaggerate and to see situations as much worse than they really are frequently leads to angry feelings. We often use colourful and exaggerated language to describe events: 'I nearly died when I realized she had heard what I said'; 'There was an absolute disaster today when the system crashed and we couldn't get the figures out in time.' Perhaps we are hardly aware that we are presenting comparatively minor events as if they are major catastrophes, and it is probably true that many of us are just using figures of speech. However, being locked into patterns of thought that turn disappointments and setbacks into full-blown disasters is a condition that fuels and feeds angry feelings. Making things much worse than they really are is illogical and unrealistic, and can have damaging effects on work and relationships. Lynn's attitude to Damian is shaped by her perception that his behaviour is appalling; she is unlikely to be able to communicate constructively with him about the situation or indeed about any other aspect of their working lives – she will turn everything into a confirmation of her exaggerated assessment of the problem.

Of course, we all enjoy making the most of a story, and work would be a lot duller if we could not exchange lively and vigorous accounts of the day's events and of our own and our colleagues' behaviour and attitudes. For many of us, having a good moan is part and parcel of the working day, and it does us good. The same is true of workplace gossip. It is an integral and enjoyable aspect of life at work, and can have a positive effect by bringing people together and fostering a sense of community. Problems arise when these types of behaviour create or reinforce angry thoughts and feelings. The activities in the book will help you to identify and deal with ways of thinking and behaving that can trigger anger, yours or someone else's.

The way it should be

Strong beliefs about the way the world should be and the way people should behave can cause you to experience anger and frustration when you feel that your values are being violated. You might have strong ideas about fairness, for example, or about what is acceptable language in the workplace. You might have a number of private rules that govern your behaviour. Your personal code of behaviour will have evolved as you adopt ideas, consciously or unconsciously, from your family, friends, significant role models and others who influence you. Some of these inherited ideas may not be appropriate for you and the world in which you work, but they influence your

ACTIVITY 6: Blips and crises

Do you turn a blip into a world crisis? Think about your use of words and phrases which exaggerate the awfulness of a situation. You could ask a friend to give you feedback – we are not always aware of how we speak and behave.

Tick the column to show how often you use the following expressions about bad situations at work. You could add your own examples.

	Never	Sometimes	Often
Awful	☐	☐	☐
Terrible	☐	☐	☐
Dreadful	☐	☐	☐
Could have died	☐	☐	☐
Catastrophe	☐	☐	☐
Disaster	☐	☐	☐
Worst possible	☐	☐	☐
Calamity	☐	☐	☐
Can't stand it when	☐	☐	☐
Drives me crazy	☐	☐	☐
Your ideas:			
_____	☐	☐	☐
_____	☐	☐	☐

reactions and contribute to your anger. These beliefs might be very close to your heart, but it is not realistic to expect others to share them, or for you to expect to be able to impose your views on other people. But even though it is unrealistic, you may become angry when there is a mismatch between what you think should happen and what does actually happen.

Lynn has definite views about how people should use their time at work, and Damian's behaviour offends her own work ethic. 'It's not right,' she says. 'He should use his own time and equipment for personal stuff.' Her feelings that Damian should live by her principles make her susceptible to anger.

Those who share Lynn's point of view may feel angry with colleagues who behave in ways that go against their beliefs about what is right and wrong. The issues in question are not always huge moral dilemmas, but can be seen in everyday matters such as the frequency and length of cigarette breaks, or requests to stay late to finish an important piece of work. You may have strong beliefs about, for example, matters of courtesy, or matters of time keeping, which could make you vulnerable to feelings of hostility. If you find that you get annoyed and worked up when people behave in ways that contradict your ideas about what is right and wrong, then it could be that your anger has its roots in your belief that the world should operate in a certain way, and that people should behave according to your moral code. Of course there is nothing wrong with having firm principles and beliefs. However, it can become harmful when you feel that everyone should follow your rules, and that these rules are universally agreed guidelines rather than your own individual choice.

Everyone's against me

We can create angry feelings for ourselves by assuming that we know the reasons for people's behaviour. When the background to an action is not clear-cut, we opt for a negative interpretation. Our interpretation of people's actions and behaviour is based on the assumption that they are being deliberately hurtful, malicious or offensive.

Scene 4: Tim's missed meeting

Tim rushes along the corridor to the meeting room, rehearsing to himself the arguments that he has prepared against the proposed changes to procedure. The changes will affect his team's workload, and he wants to present a good case for finding another solution to the problem. He arrives in good time, five minutes before the meeting is scheduled to begin, and is surprised to find that the room is empty. When no-one else turns up, Tim phones Alec, the chair of the meeting.

'Didn't Gina tell you?' says Alec. 'We had to reschedule the meeting at the last minute. We had it first thing this morning. I thought it was strange that you weren't there. But Gina put forward a persuasive case for your point of view.'

'I'm pleased about that,' says Tim through gritted teeth. He is furious with Gina. She must have deliberately not told him about the change of time so that she would be able to speak in his place at the meeting. He can feel his heart beating faster just thinking about it. He can't believe that she could be so manipulative.

ACTIVITY 7: Shoulds and oughts

(a) Check out your own shoulds and oughts. Complete the following two sentences with as many examples as you like:

At work, I think that people should . . .
At work, I think that people should not . . .

You could use these prompts to help you to focus on your beliefs about how people should behave:

sexist jokes	racist jokes
allocation of praise and blame	appropriation of praise
personal use of phone and email	acceptance of responsibility for mistakes
gossip	lying to cover up mistakes
fairness	reliability
ambition	expression of feelings
poaching customers or clients	showing appreciation
people taking home office supplies for their own use	competing for resources
	competing for promotion

(b) It could be that ingrained ideas about your own behaviour contribute to your feeling angry with yourself when you don't live up to your self-imposed ideals. Use the following prompts to help you to identify the standards that you set yourself:

being first	being helpful
working long hours	showing emotions in public
letting people down	position and authority
being in control	being hurtful
making mistakes	honesty

Complete the following two sentences with as many examples as you like:

At work, I think that I should . . .
At work, I think that I should not . . .

Tim automatically assumes the worst about the situation. He does not know the background or how it came about that he did not receive the message. You might be able to think of several possibilities. Was Gina actually instructed to give him the information? Could Alec himself have forgotten to tell Tim, and implicated Gina to cover up his mistake? Is it certain that Gina manoeuvred the situation for her own ends? Without checking that his assumptions are correct, Tim attributes malicious motives to Gina. His tendency to interpret events negatively makes him angry. Think about Lynn in Scene 1. As she sees it, Damian is abusing the system for his own ends. Her angry feelings might diminish or disappear if she discovered, for example, that the personal emails and phone calls that are taking up his time are to do with the process of arranging nursing care for his elderly parent.

Of course, in both these situations, further exploration could reveal that the assessments made by Tim and Lynn are correct. In that case, they could use the four-step plan discussed in Chapter 3 as a guide to examining the source of their anger and dealing with their angry feelings.

It is someone's fault

Another kind of thinking that leads to anger is the tendency to blame either others or yourself for things that go wrong, even when it is no one's fault. Blaming somebody else is a way of avoiding taking responsibility for our own feelings, and it results in anger and resentment. Blaming yourself turns your anger inwards, and this reaction can become a destructive habit which prevents healthy relationships and responses.

Blame is a powerful precursor to anger. Some aspects of the blaming process are based on: expectations; rigid ideas; and applying labels.

Expectations

If your expectations are unrealistic, your disappointment with yourself can lead to anger. You blame yourself for not living up to your own high standards. For example, if you pride yourself on always being accurate, or on never losing a sale, or on always meeting deadlines, you are setting yourself unrealistic and probably unattainable goals. Frustration and disappointment make you angry with yourself for failing to live up to your own demands.

It works the other way, as well. Low expectations of yourself can lead to continued lack of self-esteem and negative feelings about

ACTIVITY 8: Assuming the worst

Do you jump to conclusions about people's behaviour? Perhaps you are in the habit of thinking that people are against you. With the following situations, decide if you would instinctively have negative thoughts about the intentions and attitudes of the other person or people involved. You could add any situations that you have experienced.

	Yes	No	Perhaps
Someone causes you to spill coffee on your work station.	☐	☐	☐
Someone causes you to spill coffee on a report you have just finished.	☐	☐	☐
You don't get the promotion you wanted.	☐	☐	☐
You are criticized unjustly.	☐	☐	☐
You are criticized with justification.	☐	☐	☐
Someone misses a deadline, causing you extra work.	☐	☐	☐
Someone interrupts you in a meeting.	☐	☐	☐
A colleague does not return your greeting.	☐	☐	☐

Your ideas:

	Yes	No	Perhaps
_____	☐	☐	☐
_____	☐	☐	☐

yourself, which can make you very vulnerable to angry feelings. If you expect the worst, you are likely to get the worst, and your anger will be fed. If you have negative expectations of someone's behaviour, you are primed for anger even before anything has happened.

Rigid ideas

Another way of thinking that can fuel angry thoughts is the tendency to see things in black and white. Examples of a rigid frame of mind are believing that things are definitely right or definitely wrong, that something definitely must happen or must not happen, or that

ACTIVITY 9: *The need to blame*

(a) Do you tend to blame yourself for things that are not your fault? Tick the descriptions that apply to your behaviour. Add any other examples that occur to you.

	Sometimes	Often
You feel angry with yourself if you are late because of traffic hold-ups.	☐	☐
You apologize when someone bumps into you.	☐	☐
You feel that it is in some way your fault if you lose your job or don't get promotion.	☐	☐
You think that you must have done something wrong if someone snaps at you.	☐	☐
You say things like 'It's my own fault for being so . . .'	☐	☐

Your ideas:

_____	☐	☐
_____	☐	☐

(b) Do you tend to look for someone to blame when things go wrong? Tick the situations that apply to you. Add any other examples that occur to you.

	Sometimes	Often
A meeting you have spent time preparing for is cancelled.	☐	☐
A client takes his business elsewhere.	☐	☐
A traffic jam delays you.	☐	☐
The machine you are working on breaks down.	☐	☐

Your ideas:

_____	☐	☐
_____	☐	☐

someone definitely should or should not behave in a certain way. When you are faced with a situation that contradicts your set ideas, you feel extremely uncomfortable and cannot adapt your approach. Your instinct may be to vent your anger in blaming someone or something – the other person, yourself, your managers at work, the firm, society, the world . . .

Applying labels

This kind of negative thinking prevents you from seeing the whole person or the whole situation. Instead, you fix on an aspect that annoys you, and do the mental equivalent of writing this aspect on a Post-It note and sticking it on to your image of the person (the person of course could be yourself). All you see is that one quality. Every time you encounter the person or the situation, you kick-start your anger. You disregard the positive aspects and move into blaming mode.

Approaches to Anger

Our behaviour when we are angry is an expression of thoughts and feelings. Understanding your own response in each area – feeling, behaviour and thinking – will help you to learn how to manage angry feelings effectively. Psychologists and therapists offer different approaches to the roles played by these three components. Psychoanalysts developing the work of Sigmund Freud (1856–1939) draw attention to the emotions that govern our behaviour. Their work helps us to understand, for example, how anger is linked to the stress or anxiety we feel when our needs or self-esteem are threatened. The Freudian approach also highlights the way our defence mechanisms work, causing us to transfer or project our angry emotions on to something other than the true source. Behaviourists, such as B. F. Skinner (1904–99), focus on how past behaviour influences current behaviour, and on how our behaviour is related to its consequences and effects. This theory explores the link between what has gone before, the way we behave and what happens as a result of our behaviour. Our behaviour will change if the antecedent (what has happened before) and the consequences change.

In more recent years, cognitive psychology has brought another slant to the study of mental processes. Cognitive psychologists believe that our thoughts influence our emotions. Our feelings are not an automatic response to an event that provokes or triggers our anger; we can control and alter our feelings by thinking more realistically about the event. The work of Aaron Beck (1921–), who focuses on the kind of distorted thinking that leads to negative feelings, and Albert Ellis (1913–), whose development of Rational Emotive Therapy describes how irrational beliefs and faulty ways of thinking can produce anger and frustration, offers essential insights into this approach to anger management. This therapy emphasizes individuals' capacity for creating their own emotions, and gives tools for changing our thoughts, attitudes, self-concept, motivation and expectations. The key to our anger is in our interpretation of events, not in the events themselves. After all, different people can react differently to the same provocation. We make ourselves angry, and we can make ourselves less angry by changing our thinking and our beliefs.

> Everything is what your opinion makes it, and that opinion lies with yourself.
>
> *Marcus Aurelius*

The important thing to realize is that there is an element of choice in how we experience and express anger, and we are better equipped to exercise that choice if we are aware of the basis of our angry emotions and the triggers that activate them. The feelings that drive our emotional response have their roots in our basic needs and in our individual emotional history. You are now aware of some of the mental and emotional causes of anger. The next chapter helps you to examine how you usually behave when you are angry and how you usually cope with your angry feelings. Once you have identified your personal anger profile, you will be able to move on to learn the steps to take that will help you to manage your feelings and behaviour effectively.

ANSWERS TO ACTIVITY 1

1 True 2 False 3 True 4 True 5 True 6 False 7 True 8 False 9 False 10 False

As you read the book, keep track of your responses by filling in the chart below. Use your quiz answers as a basis.

My old ideas about anger   *My new ideas about anger*

_____   _____

_____   _____

_____   _____

_____   _____

_____   _____

_____   _____

2

Your Personal Pattern of Anger

How do you respond when you feel angry? We have already noted that people react in different ways when their anger is provoked. Your way of responding depends on your personality and your personal history. Our childhood experiences, cultural backgrounds and environment influence our anger patterns, and by the time we reach adulthood we have developed ways of dealing with anger that seem to be an ingrained part of our personalities. This chapter will help you to identify your behaviour and the ideas and experiences on which it is based.

ACTIVITY 10: What I do when I'm angry

The following questions will help you to identify your way of managing angry feelings. Tick one box for each response.

When I feel angry I:

	Often	Sometimes	Never
1 shout or speak very loudly	☐	☐	☐
2 become physically aggressive	☐	☐	☐
3 become verbally aggressive	☐	☐	☐
4 feel that my reactions are caused by being hurt or upset	☐	☐	☐
5 feel that my reactions are caused by being disappointed	☐	☐	☐
6 switch off	☐	☐	☐
7 bottle it up	☐	☐	☐
8 walk away	☐	☐	☐
9 hope it will go away	☐	☐	☐
10 take my feelings out on someone else	☐	☐	☐
11 don't say anything, but bang a door, or storm out	☐	☐	☐
12 show my displeasure with my body language	☐	☐	☐

	Often	Sometimes	Never
13 complain to other people	☐	☐	☐
14 find a way of getting back at the person	☐	☐	☐

If you have ticked the 'never' box for every question, you may already be well on the way to managing your anger effectively. If you have ticked several 'often' or 'sometimes' boxes, it is likely that you are not dealing healthily with your anger. You might be using one or more of the strategies described below, which seem to be ways of coping with angry feelings, but which do not confront the situation productively.

Letting it out

Most of us will have experienced the expressions of anger described in Questions 1–3, either in our own behaviour or at the receiving end of someone else's. (Chapter 5 looks at how to deal with someone else's anger.) This is the kind of behaviour that often arises from the heat of the moment. Such outbursts can be frightening and disturbing for everyone involved, and can lead to feelings of guilt and remorse. Lashing out is not an effective way to meet people's needs in the workplace, even if the expression of anger might feel good in the short term, in that it gives release to pent-up feelings. Flying off the handle is essentially a destructive way of handling difficult situations, and leads to an atmosphere of fear and intimidation. You are letting your anger control you, and neglecting to take responsibility for your actions.

Shutting it off

Questions 4–5 focus on ways in which we repress our angry feelings. Repression means that we do not acknowledge our anger, but rather we deny its existence. It is buried in the unconscious part of the mind, and affects our behaviour without our realizing it. Physically, you experience an angry response, but you find other explanations for your feelings.

Keeping it in

This is to do with suppressing feelings. The reactions described in Questions 6–9 are examples of ways in which we choose not to express our anger. You know that you are angry, but you try to ignore it. You might behave in this way because you feel uncomfortable about expressing strong negative emotions. It could be that you would like to communicate your feelings but are not sure how to, or are scared that you will deliver one of the angry outbursts referred to above, or burst into tears. Lack of confidence in your ability to express your feelings while maintaining good relationships and professional credibility means that you bottle them up instead of expressing them appropriately. A possible consequence of suppressing anger is that strong feelings build up until they emerge in a violent explosion of anger which is far more damaging than it would have been to acknowledge your feelings and express them appropriately. Suppressed anger, like buried anger, can also lead to depression as your negative emotions are turned in on yourself instead of being focused on outside events.

Kicking the cat

Many of us have been in a situation where we take out our feelings on an innocent person or object, as described in Question 10. Unable or unwilling to deal with a person or situation directly, we bottle up our emotion until we can vent it in a way that we feel is safe, displacing our anger onto something or someone that is less threatening than the real object of our annoyance. We usually know when we are doing this, or realize shortly afterwards what we have done, and may feel guilty about it. You might notice how Lynn in Scene 1 snaps at Oliver instead of dealing directly with Damian, the real object of her anger.

Some schools of thought suggest that it is helpful to vent anger in a safe way, such as punching a cushion or writing an angry letter then tearing it up. Releasing your feelings in this way can be cathartic, and can prevent your anger from building up. On the other hand, such activities legitimize hostility and do not address the roots and causes of the angry feelings. A healthier way of releasing your angry energy would be to engage in some physical activity such as running or vigorous walking in which you are not directing your feelings on to a specific object.

Giving the cold shoulder

Questions 11 and 12 illustrate another kind of indirect response, where we make it clear that we are annoyed with somebody or something without directly confronting the person or issue. Just as Bina in Scene 3 is offhand and rude with Sue, communicating her anger with cold and unfriendly behaviour, so we move into withdrawal mode in which we make it known that something is wrong, but we do not attack the person concerned or communicate what it is that is bothering us. You might, for example, make it clear that you are ignoring the person with whom you are angry, or you might slam down tools or equipment, or mutter under your breath.

Stabbing in the back

The behaviours described in Questions 13 and 14 are other examples of how we sometimes deal with our anger indirectly. We get back at the person involved by employing tactics which are pretty underhand, such as spreading rumours, or making anonymous complaints. You might do things like not passing on information, or you may even deliberately mess up work on which the person is depending. Some workers have admitted to tactics such as leaving a computer virus on a co-worker's disk. Assistants who are angry with their bosses use various strategies to embarrass and humiliate the offenders. For example, they make sure that sensitive items of personal correspondence are accidentally left in a public place. One disgruntled assistant placed an ad in a lonely hearts column with her boss's home phone number.

Why these strategies do not work

Although some of the behaviour we have just discussed might seem to be a good idea, perhaps because it meets your immediate needs, whether they be to let off steam or to avoid confrontation, these are not effective ways of managing anger. From a professional point of view, you are not dealing with the issues that concern you. Unless you can clearly express what is bothering you, there is no chance that the work situation will get any better.

Not only this, but venting anger in these indirect ways only breeds more anger. The more you are in an angry state, the more you grow used to it, and you find that responding angrily becomes a habit. You become hooked on it, probably not realizing that you are trading short-term satisfaction for long-term disaster. There are serious consequences of allowing hostile feelings to influence your behaviour negatively, instead of expressing them healthily and positively.

Emotional cost

The emotional cost of living with anger is high. The cycle of angry thoughts and actions can lead to uncomfortable feelings of tension, frustration, guilt, remorse, inadequacy. It can damage your self-esteem and ruin your personal and professional relationships. Anger which is turned inwards through suppression or repression can result in you becoming depressed.

Mental effects

Anger can affect your mental processes in many ways. It can cause you to have difficulty in concentrating and can affect your decision-making ability. If you are frequently tense and wound-up you cannot think straight, and find it difficult to focus on your work. If your mind is filled with angry and anxious thoughts you are limiting your potential to be creative and to find solutions to problems.

Effects on behaviour

The effects of mismanaged anger may be seen in people's behaviour. It might cause you to be restless and edgy; it might lead you into behaviour which is compulsive or obsessive. Some people's dependence on drugs or stimulants has its roots in unresolved anger. It can affect the way you relate to others, causing you perhaps to become isolated or withdrawn.

Effects on work

We have already looked at some of the ways in which anger can affect work and working relationships. Mismanaged anger causes a range of negative effects, such as poor motivation, breakdowns in communication, dissatisfaction, unacceptably high rates of job turnover, personal and professional disputes. Lack of self-esteem, a consequence of mismanaged anger, may result in you not achieving your potential at work. You may be unwilling to make yourself visible or promote your own interests, and other people may take you at your own self-evaluation and overlook you.

ACTIVITY 11: How anger affects your life

Think about how anger affects your life at the moment, and about its possible long-term effects if it is not managed properly. Jot down some responses under each of the following headings.

YOUR PERSONAL PATTERN OF ANGER

Relationships

Give four examples of how anger affects your relationships with others.

1 _____

2 _____

3 _____

4 _____

Emotional health

Give four examples of uncomfortable or unwelcome
feelings caused by anger.

1 _____

2 _____

3 _____

4 _____

Mental abilities

Give four examples of how anger affects your ability to think.

1 _____

2 _____

3 _____

4 _____

YOUR PERSONAL PATTERN OF ANGER

Behaviour

Give some examples of how anger affects the way you behave.

1 _____

2 _____

3 _____

4 _____

Working life
Give four examples of how anger may affect your career.

1 _____

2 _____

3 _____

4 _____

_____

Your anger history

Your personal history through childhood and your adult life will have shaped your attitude to the experience of anger. You may have learnt certain ways of expressing or not expressing emotion that influence your behaviour now. Also, you may still be carrying the burden of unresolved anger from the distant or recent past. Use the following prompts to help you to identify habits of thought and behaviour that could be affecting your ability to manage anger effectively.

ACTIVITY 12: When I was young

(a) Make notes under the following headings. Focus on the way that you felt and the way that you behaved, and how your behaviour was punished or rewarded.

How I responded to the anger of parents

Situation _____

What happened? _____

What was the result? _____

Situation _____

What happened? _____

What was the result? _____

How I responded to the anger of other authority figures

Situation _____

What happened? _____

What was the result? _____

Situation _____

What happened? _____

What was the result? _____

YOUR PERSONAL PATTERN OF ANGER

How adults responded to my shows of temper or anger

Situation _____

What happened? _____

What was the result? _____

Situation _____

What happened? _____

What was the result? _____

(b) Some of your attitudes to anger and how it is expressed may have been picked up in your early life. Tick any of the following beliefs that reflect your ideas about anger. Next to each one, write a belief that is more appropriate for your adult management of anger.

Old thought	*New thought*
Getting angry is a sign of weakness.	_____
It is important not to upset people.	_____
It is a good thing to keep 'a stiff upper lip'.	_____
Anger should be kept to yourself.	_____
Expressions of anger create an unpleasant atmosphere.	_____
No-one listens unless you get angry.	_____

_____

Anger patterns carried over from childhood

It is possible that anger from your earlier life is affecting the way you deal with your emotions now. Your experiences with authority figures, for example, may influence the way you respond to your managers or bosses. If your childhood expressions of anger were greeted with amusement or dismissed, you might not feel able to express angry feelings to someone in authority over you now. On the other hand, if you were unable to communicate your anger, but instead took on the role of peacemaker, you might still have difficulty with expressing negative feelings.

ACTIVITY 13: Lasting influence

(a) Think about situations in which your early experience of expressing or receiving anger influences your present behaviour.

Dealing with	*Early experience/influence*	*How I behave now*
my manager		
team members		
criticism		
customers/clients		
meetings		
bullying		
racism		
sexism		
other people's success		
negotiating		

Your ideas:

(b) Now think about the way you would like to behave in some of these situations.

Dealing with   *How I would like to behave*

1 _____

2 _____

3 _____

4 _____

_____

Adult anger experiences

You might be aware of feelings of hurt or hostility stemming from situations in your more recent adult life that you have not dealt with satisfactorily. There may be issues to do with people or events that still get to you, because you did not manage your anger at the time.

_____

ACTIVITY 14: Old wounds

(a) Think about any situations you have experienced about which you felt angry at the time, and which still arouse angry feelings.

	How I felt at time	*How I feel now*
Being treated unfairly		
Not being thanked		
Not being appreciated		
Jokes being made at your expense		
Being taken for granted		

How I felt at time   *How I feel now*

Being let down   _____

Your ideas:

_____

_____

(b) Choose three of the above situations which arouse the strongest response in you. Describe how you feel about each one. Then describe how you would like to feel.

Situation   *How I feel*   *How I would like to feel*

1 _____

2 _____

3 _____

_____

You can deal constructively with a backlog of unresolved anger. Bringing out your feelings into the open is the first step to dealing with them. If this aspect of your emotional responses is a real problem and remains so even after you have worked on suggestions for how to manage your anger, you might find it helpful to talk to a professional therapist.

Your body's response to anger

Anger is a positive physical reaction that prepares us to deal with threat. When we perceive a dangerous challenge to our well-being, our brain clicks into action and sends messages to other parts of the body to prepare for action. Our physical responses when we feel angry are caused by the same processes that apply when we are frightened, or when we are about to take part in vigorous physical activity, for example, in a competitive sport. Our bodies gear up to give us the physical energy needed to meet the challenge, be it by fighting the enemy, running for our lives or beating the other team. We are ready for 'fight or flight'. Adrenalin is released into the blood-stream, and the liver produces glucose to give the muscles the fuel that they need. All the body's functions are channelled into producing the required energy. This is why when you feel very angry you breathe more quickly, have tense muscles and a fast-beating heart, a dry mouth and uncomfortable stomach. What has happened is that in order to supply your muscles with the energy that they need, your heart has been beating faster to pump the oxygen-bearing blood more quickly, blood has been diverted from your digestive system, causing it to close down and your saliva to dry up, and your body has cooled itself by perspiring in anticipation of the heat that will be generated by physical action.

This is fine when the energy is expended through physical action and your body returns to normal. Your system has been prepared for a temporary spurt of action, after which your body calms down. You do not need the same degree of energy, so your glucose level drops. Your heart stops thumping, and your muscles relax. Your digestive system comes back into play. Your body has helped you to express your anger appropriately, and now normal service is resumed.

Unfortunately, this healthy process is often abused. We cannot physically fight or run away, so we remain in a state of arousal with

---

ACTIVITY 15: Health check

The following physical conditions might be caused by anger. Check to see how often and how severely you suffer from them.

	Often	Very often	Severe	Very severe
Hypertension	☐	☐	☐	☐
Stomach upsets	☐	☐	☐	☐
Ulcers	☐	☐	☐	☐
Headaches	☐	☐	☐	☐
Gastritis	☐	☐	☐	☐
Digestive problems	☐	☐	☐	☐
Muscle pain	☐	☐	☐	☐
Feeling shaky	☐	☐	☐	☐
Feeling on edge	☐	☐	☐	☐

no outlet for our energy. If we frequently get into a state of angry arousal, or if this state is sustained for long periods of time, then we are likely to experience a range of physical disorders. If your muscles are constantly tensed, ready for exertion, you are likely to suffer from aches and pains and inflammatory disorders. If your body constantly produces glucose you could find that you have excess sugar in your blood. The constant presence of acid in your digestive system could well lead to gastric and digestive problems. It is highly likely that you will develop high blood pressure, caused by your blood vessels being constricted by the production of the hormone noradrenalin (norepinephrine U.S.) which is pumped out during an angry response. This can lead to heart attacks and strokes, and may prove to be fatal.

More about your body

Other physical conditions can cause you to respond with anger or irritation in situations which in different circumstances would not have the same effect.

Scene 5: Deepak's sleepless nights

Deepak has almost finished drawing up the rotas for the next month. All he needs is for Rachel to confirm her holiday arrangements, then he can distribute the chart. He wonders whether he should email a reminder to Rachel, and decides not to. She did say she would get back to him by the end of the day. Deepak yawns and stretches, and rubs his eyes. He has felt tired all week, sometimes almost dropping off to sleep at his desk. Everyone had laughingly warned him about the broken nights once the baby arrived, but he'd had no idea that lack of sleep would affect him like this.

'Deepak?' Rachel is at his desk. 'Look, I'm really sorry, but I won't be able to give you those dates until tomorrow. But I'll get them to you first thing, I promise.'

Deepak explodes. 'That's just not good enough! Do you know how hard I've worked on these rotas? I wanted to get them out before I went home, but now you've held everything up. Just don't assume that you'll get the dates you want, that's all. I can't guarantee anything now.'

Rachel is upset, and doesn't know why Deepak is speaking to her like that. He doesn't usually have such a short fuse. Later, Deepak is angry with himself for having been angry with Rachel. If he hadn't felt so exhausted he would have spoken very differently to her. That's the trouble with being over-tired, you feel so edgy that all your judgement disappears. He will have to make it right with Rachel, if he can.

ACTIVITY 16: Physical conditions

Think about the particular physical states and conditions that increase your likelihood of snapping or responding angrily. Draw a circle around any here that apply to you, and add any others.

feeling over-tired	having a headache
muscle pain	being too hot
being too cold	being hungry
going through hormonal changes	longing for caffeine
longing for a cigarette	getting over a virus

ACTIVITY 17: Your anger profile

Fill in the chart to get an overview of your anger response. Use the ideas in the first two chapters to help you to identify the beliefs and ideas that influence the way you feel and behave.

Situation	What I thought	Underlying belief	What I felt	What I did
1				
2				
3				
4				
5				
6				

Your response to anger is a learned response. It is not easy to change well-established patterns of thought and behaviour, but you can learn new ways of dealing with anger and hostility. Move on now to find out how to make choices that enable you to change the way you think about people and situations, and to manage your emotions and behaviour more effectively.

3

Four-Step Plan for Dealing with Anger

Step one: acknowledge your feelings

The first step to managing anger is admitting that you are feeling angry. There are two issues here – the first is acknowledging that it is anger that you are experiencing, and not the variety of emotions that are associated with it, and the second is owning that the emotion is your own and not a feeling that is imposed on you by something or someone else. Anger that is acknowledged and out in the open is far less destructive than hidden or repressed hostility. But many of us have developed ways to avoid taking responsibility for this uncomfortable emotion, and we employ a range of tactics and behaviours that allows us to deny the anger that we feel.

Scene 6: Charlotte's long lunch breaks

Liz says that it doesn't bother her that her co-worker Charlotte gets away with taking very long lunch breaks. Charlotte always has an amusing story to explain her tardy return to the studio, and their manager Debbie just laughs and says that Charlotte will have to stay late to make up the lost time, but Charlotte never does.

One day when Charlotte returns from her lunch break Liz says, 'Oh, you've just missed the new art director. He wanted to meet us both.'

Charlotte frowns. 'When was this arranged? I didn't know.'

Liz shrugs apologetically. 'Last week sometime. I must have just forgotten to tell you. I'm really sorry, Charlotte.'

Liz may say that she is really sorry, and she may believe that she is. But what Liz is really feeling is anger. Unless she recognizes and accepts this, she will not deal with the situation effectively, but will continue to 'forget' to pass on information, or find other ways of denying that she is angry.

Ways of not owning our feelings

There are several tactics that we employ to avoid owning our feelings.

It's not happening

You may avoid responsibility for your feelings by denying that you have them. Sometimes we duck away from facing the strength of our feelings by diminishing them. We refuse to admit that we feel angry, and find other, more acceptable ways of identifying our feelings. You might habitually describe your feelings of anger in phrases such as 'cheesed off' that do not express the nature or extent of your feelings, and which are in fact a form of denial although they appear to acknowledge your emotional state.

Games people play

Another way of denying angry feelings is to draw other people on to your side and lead them to agree with your way of seeing the situation. You enter into a kind of collusive game which helps you to avoid the truth of your feelings. A similar tactic is to put up with a situation you do not like, telling yourself that it's not so bad, so that you do not have to accept the responsibility for managing your feelings.

It's you, not me

Blaming other people for your own negative feelings is a common way of refusing to accept responsibility for ourselves. We do this when we use expressions such as 'He makes me angry' or 'It makes me angry.' This tactic pushes the focus away from ourselves on to external factors, and we can tell ourselves that it's not our fault that we feel this way because something or someone else is forcing us to react angrily.

Avoiding the issue

We can pretend that a situation does not exist simply by avoiding it. Rather than acknowledge the angry feelings that are engendered at a certain meeting, for example, we find reasons not to attend the meeting. Rather than accepting that we feel angry with someone's behaviour, we try not to have anything to do with that person.

Reason not emotion

Sometimes we feel more comfortable talking about thoughts than about emotions. So we rationalize our feelings, saying things like 'I don't think she should have behaved like that' or 'It's not right to treat people that way.' These phrases may be perfectly valid responses to what has happened, but they do not express how you are feeling. Remember, anger is not an intellectual process, it is an emotion.

How to own your feelings

Decide exactly what emotion you are experiencing. Identifying the precise nature and degree of your angry response is a crucial first step to managing it. Think about the level of your anger – you might find that your anger is less than you think, or you might find that you are in fact more deeply angry than you first thought. You have to realize the nature of your feelings before you can make decisions about how to deal with them. There is a range of words to describe different aspects and different degrees of anger. You will find it helpful to find the right word or phrase to describe just how strong your feelings are.

Use 'I' statements to own and acknowledge your feelings. Tell yourself 'I am feeling angry'; 'I feel frustrated.' Do not suppress or deny your feelings; do not try to blame someone or something else for what is your own emotional response. You could practise saying these statements aloud to yourself, or try any method you like to become comfortable and familiar with claiming your feelings.

ACTIVITY 18: Describing angry feelings

(a) List six occasions on which you felt angry. For each situation, choose the most appropriate word or phrase from the list on p.41 to describe your feelings. Use words of your own if you prefer.

Situation   *Feeling*

1 _____

2 _____

3 _____

4 _____

5 _____

6 _____

annoyed	frustrated	niggled	furious	very annoyed
livid	irritated	disgusted	mildly frustrated	resentful
indignant	raging	exasperated	nettled	worked up
beside myself with anger	peeved			

(b) Use the situations and words that you identified, and turn each one into a statement that acknowledges your feelings. Change the first part of the sentence where appropriate.

1 When _____ happens/happened, I feel/felt _____

2 _____

3 _____

4 _____

5 _____

6 _____

Step two: identify the source

Think of what it is that you are angry about. It may not be the situation or person which is facing you at the moment. You may be angry because of the present situation, or because of something to do with your past, or because of some combination of past and present issues. It is important to identify the source of your anger so that you can take steps to deal with it.

Scene 7: Gail's angry with someone

Gail is having a tough day. It began badly when she told Rob that she would not be able to go to his firm's dinner because she had a school meeting on the same evening. Then she got off to a late start because the childminder didn't arrive on time, and she got caught in the heavy traffic along the bypass. As she rushes towards her classroom the deputy head teacher approaches her with an apologetic look that spells trouble.

'Sorry, Gail,' he says. 'I've had to put you down to cover a class this morning.'

'But that was my only free period! I'd planned to order some stock – I don't know when I'm going to get a chance to do it now! You keep doing this to me!'

Fuming, Gail starts the lesson and asks for last night's homework to be handed in. When Jade Jarrow says that she has not done the work, Gail sees red. She tells Jade off in no uncertain terms, and takes every opportunity during the rest of the day to tell anyone who will listen about Jade's attitude problem and how angry it makes her.

Gail thinks that she is angry with Jade. In fact, Jade is not the real object of her anger, and in different circumstances she probably would not have reacted so strongly to Jade's not having done her homework. Gail has to think hard about who is the real source of her annoyance. She has been in a conflict situation with Rob, with the childminder and with the deputy head. When she thinks it through and tests out her feelings, she realizes that the person with whom she is angry is her childminder, who has been becoming less reliable. Now that Gail has identified the source of her anger, she can decide what to do about it – and she can also plan how to re-establish a relationship with Jade.

ACTIVITY 19: Who are you angry with?

Think about some occasions on which you felt angry with someone. In each case, go back over the situations and decide if the person with whom you felt angry was in fact the real source of your hostile feelings.

Situation   Person with whom I felt angry   Possible true source of feelings

1 _____

2 _____

3 _____

4 _____

Get the right issue

Sometimes it is not easy to identify the real issue which is the source of angry feelings. It is easier, sometimes, to be angry about inefficient public transport, or an untidy office, or a demand for extra work than it is to face what is really at the core of our emotional response. After all, it is perfectly reasonable to feel irritated and annoyed by situations such as these, and everyone will sympathize with our feelings. But if you find you keep getting angry about these issues, or if your feelings are stronger than the situation really justifies, or if you find that they constantly niggle away at you, think about what is the true object of your feelings. It is possible that the matter which is bugging you is in fact something else, and by not recognizing it, you are venting your anger on the wrong source.

Scene 8: Martin's bad journey

Martin grumbles more and more about his journey to work. It is not a particularly difficult journey, and he does not have far to travel, but every day he comes in with complaints about the poor car-parking facilities at the railway station, the crowded carriages, the delays. He gets quite worked up as he describes the daily journey and says how angry he is that services are so inefficient.

One day Judy says to him, 'Why don't you do something about it, if it upsets you so much? Join one of the groups who campaign for better transport.' When Martin does not respond enthusiastically to this idea, she adds, 'Or you could always look for a job that doesn't involve travel.'

These words strike a chord with Martin, and he suddenly realizes that it is not the journey to work that has been getting to him, it's the job itself. He is unhappy and frustrated in his work, but has been channelling his feelings of dissatisfaction into expressions of anger about something else. Now that Martin recognizes that the real issue is his job, he is in a position to deal with his feelings in a positive way.

ACTIVITY 20: What are you angry about?

Think of some occasions when you felt angry about something. In each case, go back over the situation and decide if the issue about which you felt angry was in fact the real source of your hostile feelings.

Situation	Issue about which I felt angry	Possible true source of feelings
1		
2		
3		
4		

Scene 9: Jenna's self-anger

Jenna smiles as she congratulates Paula. 'Well done, Paula. I think you'll make a terrific team leader.' Inside, she is seething. She cannot believe that someone as sloppy and unreliable as Paula should receive promotion. Jenna can hardly bear to look at her, and cannot get out of the room quickly enough. She phones Darren straight away.

'I'm so mad! She just doesn't deserve it! That's so typical of this place, they can't see what's in front of their noses. They're taken in by people like Paula.'

'Well, you could have applied for the position,' says Darren. 'You are just as well qualified and experienced as Paula.'

Jenna sniffs. 'I wouldn't want it anyway.'

'Of course you wouldn't,' Darren says kindly.

Jenna is angry with herself. She could have applied for the job, and didn't. Her stance that she wouldn't want it anyway is just a position that she assumes so as not to face the implications of her decision not to apply. If she had applied and had not been successful, she might still be annoyed with herself, but for different reasons. Until Jenna looks at her own behaviour and motives, she will continue to express anger about Paula and the organization instead of acknowledging the true source of her anger – herself.

ACTIVITY 21: Identify the source of your anger

Check out the source of your anger before you make any decisions about how to deal with it. When you are angry or worked up about someone or something, ask yourself:
(a) What exactly am I angry about?
(b) Who exactly am I angry with?

Step three: find solutions

Once you have identified and accepted the nature and the strength of your feelings, and attributed them to the correct source, you are in a good position to find ways of managing your anger. You are aware of your feelings and of how they are affecting you, and are able to control and manage them. You have a choice about how you behave. A number of solutions are open to you; which one you choose will depend on your individual circumstances and what you actually want to happen. You are in control. You can choose to reveal your feelings, or not; you can choose how you reveal them; you can choose what steps you take to deal with the situation.

What outcome do you want?

You may want one or more of the following:

to feel calm and in control
to express how you feel
to maintain self-respect
to maintain respect for the other person
to bring about a change in someone's behaviour
to bring about a change in a situation
not to feel angry

ACTIVITY 22: Outcomes

Choose some situations in which you feel angry. For each one, decide what you would like to happen (a) in the short term, and (b) in the long term.

Situation	*Short-term outcome*	*Long-term outcome*
1		
2		
3		
4		
5		
6		
7		
8		

How much is it worth?

The first step to finding the appropriate solution for you is to decide how much you want to go ahead with dealing with the situation. The issue might be comparatively trivial, and not worth the emotional and physical energy it would take to deal with it. It is possible to walk away from an argument or a disagreement. Even if you believe that you are in the right, it may not always be necessary to prove it. For some situations, you can avoid becoming caught up in potentially hostile and difficult exchanges by saying something like, 'Let's agree to differ about this.'

The suggestions in Activity 23 will help you to determine how important the matter is to you.

ACTIVITY 23: How much does it matter?

(a) On a scale of 1–10, with 1 being low and 10 being high, how important is this matter?

Situation   *Rating*

1 _____

2 _____

3 _____

(b) Draw a circle and in its centre mark a cross representing yourself. Where, in relation to you, is the person or situation? How close are they? How much do they matter? Think about this in terms of how much they matter to you or how much effect they will have on your life. Mark a cross to show their relative closeness or distance. If they are at the edge of your circle, it could be that this issue is not all that important to you.

Possible solution

If the issue is, in the overall scheme of things, not very important, let the anger go. Decide not to get worked up about whatever it is that is getting to you. Look at strategies to help you to stop your angry feelings and to remain calm.

> How much more grievous are the consequences of anger than the causes of it.
>
> *Marcus Aurelius*

Is my anger justified?

Remember that anger is not your enemy. It is a helpful response which gives you a warning, telling you that something is wrong and preparing you to deal with the threat. Anger lets you know that something needs to be changed, in yourself, in other people, or in the world.

> The world needs anger. The world often continues to allow evil because it isn't angry enough.
>
> *Bede Jarrett*

Your angry response may be justified. Separate yourself from the emotion, and think objectively about the situation you face. You have a right to feel angry when you are threatened or attacked, or when something or someone that you value is violated. You have a right to feel angry when you lose someone or something that you value.

ACTIVITY 24: Your anger rights

Complete this sentence with as many examples as you wish.

I have the right to feel angry when:

1 _____

2 _____

3 _____

4 _____

5 _____

6 _____

7 _____

8 _____

9 _____

10 _____

Check that your anger is based on a genuine right, and that it is not distorted by the kind of unhelpful patterns of thinking that we looked at in Chapter 1. Ask yourself:

(a) Am I applying unrealistic rules and standards?
(b) Am I sure about the intentions of the person involved?

You may need to take some steps to establish the background to someone else's behaviour. You might remember Tim in Scene 4, who is convinced that Gina deliberately withheld information about a meeting from him. Tim should first check to what extent his response to this event is shaped by his set ideas about people's behaviour. For example, he might be in the habit of assuming that people are out to do him down (the section: *Changing negative beliefs to positive ones* on pp. 50–54 gives some suggestions for how to deal with this way of thinking). Having checked that he is not jumping to a conclusion based on his own preconceptions, Tim needs to find out what Gina's motives were. If he discovers that Gina did act deliberately and maliciously, he can choose to deal with his anger in one of the ways described below. If he discovers that Gina did not intend to do him any harm, he may choose another option. Once he is sure that his reaction is not based on unrealistic or rigid ideas, and having ascertained the background to the event, Tim is in a better position to make decisions about how to deal with the situation calmly and rationally.

Possible solutions

If your anger is justified and healthy, you have some options:

(a) You can decide to express your feelings appropriately.
(b) You can decide not to express your feelings.
(c) You can decide to change the way you look at the situation.

If your anger is based on unhelpful ideas and beliefs, you have some options:

(a) You can decide to change your negative beliefs to more positive ones.
(b) You can use rational self-talk and other techniques to reduce your anger.
(c) You can decide to change the way you look at the situation.

Step four: plan your strategy

There is a variety of tactics you can use to help you to calm down and stop angry feelings before they overwhelm you. The strategies described here focus on two aspects of managing anger: expressing your anger appropriately, and changing the way that you think so that you do not get annoyed so quickly or stay annoyed for so long. The following chapter will give you some suggestions about dealing with situations which continue to get to you or which take you by surprise. Before going on to look at those coping mechanisms, think about the following ways of making fundamental differences to how you manage your angry feelings.

Changing negative beliefs to positive ones

In Chapter 1 we looked at ways in which our beliefs and our values and our assumptions about the world and the people in it can contribute to feelings of anger and hostility. If our expectations are unreasonable and unrealistic we are likely to be constantly challenged by people and events that frustrate our definition of ourselves and the world. However, you can change the way that you think, and you can channel your thoughts into a direction that will reduce the frequency and intensity of your anger. Replacing negative, unhelpful interpretations of events with more positive ways of looking at the situation will enable you to remain calm or to calm yourself down when you feel yourself beginning to respond angrily.

Changing negative beliefs requires hard work and commitment. Many of the ideas that govern our thoughts and behaviour have been ours since childhood, and we have never thought to re-examine them. Examining, questioning and where necessary changing these beliefs are major steps to controlling and managing anger.

Loosen up

Start by looking back at Activity 7, where you identified some of your ideas about the way people should and should not behave at work. You do not have to attempt to turn your way of thinking on its head, but you will find it helpful to develop a less rigid, more flexible set of beliefs. Instead of thinking in terms of what people should do and ought to do, acknowledge that although you would prefer them to behave in a certain way, it is their choice to act as they wish. Just as you have ideas and values which have been shaped by your childhood and early experience, so have they. Other people think that their behaviour and ideas are justified, just as you believe that yours are. Of course others' words and behaviour will sometimes provoke justified anger, and in those cases you will choose how to deal with your response. But by removing your own ethical and moral code from the centre of the universe you make it possible to replace easily triggered annoyance with a more measured, tolerant response.

ACTIVITY 25: Changing beliefs

Choose three of your 'shoulds and oughts' about other people and replace them with a more flexible belief. The example shows you how to do this.

Unhelpful belief	*More flexible belief*
e.g. People should not make sexist remarks.	I would prefer that people do not make sexist remarks, but I know that some people will. I can choose how I respond to this behaviour.

1 _____

2 _____

3 _____

Now choose three 'shoulds and oughts' about your own behaviour and replace them with a more flexible belief.

Unhelpful belief	*More flexible belief*

1 _____

2 _____

3 _____

Put it in perspective

If you tend to exaggerate the negative impact and importance of events, change this way of thinking and adopt an attitude that keeps things in a manageable perspective. Decide not to wind yourself up by thinking that everything is awful and as bad as it could possibly be. Decide what kind of statement you will use to express your new way of thinking. The example below shows you how you can replace thoughts about how dreadful a situation is with thoughts that will help you to develop a calm approach.

ACTIVITY 26: Be more realistic

Choose three examples from your own experience of the kind of thinking that makes things much worse than they really are. For each example, come up with a statement that puts the situation in a more realistic perspective.

Thought that leads to angry feelings *Thought that leads to calm feelings*

e.g. The way my manager speaks to me is absolutely appalling.

The way my manager speaks to me can be thoughtless and insensitive. War and famine are appalling, not her behaviour.

1 _____

2 _____

3 _____

They might not mean it

If you have a tendency to believe that the world is against you, and that people's behaviour shows a deliberate intention to harm you in some way, then your anger will be easily and frequently triggered. Of course you would not wish to be naïve and to leave yourself vulnerable to office politicking, and if someone is really showing you antagonism, you should raise the matter with the person concerned. But if you are in the habit of assuming the worst, then developing a more considered assessment of others' actions and motives will actually lead to more effective communication as well as helping you to keep calm. After all, you can probably think of times when your own behaviour may have been open to misinterpretation. Many of us have experienced being so absorbed in our own work or thoughts that we have not noticed someone greeting us or smiling at us. We have all had off days when we have appeared grumpy and bad-tempered to other people without realizing the impression that we are creating.

ACTIVITY 27: Alternative explanations

Look at the situation below, and come up with different interpretations of Guy's behaviour. Then identify three occasions when your anger with someone reflected your belief that the person deliberately meant to hurt or inconvenience you. Think of as many different reasons as you can for their behaviour.

Situation	My underlying belief at the time	Other explanations
Feeling angry when Guy did not return my greeting	Guy deliberately snubbed me	

1 _____

2 _____

3 _____

No-one's fault

The urge to find someone or something to blame when things go wrong can be, as we have seen, a negative and anger-inducing instinct. Of course issues of accountability and responsibility need to be addressed, but in some situations the search for blame is irrelevant and unproductive, and blaming others for your feelings is a way of avoiding taking responsibility for yourself. Replace your belief that it must be someone else's fault with a statement along the lines of: It is bad/annoying/frustrating that this has happened, but since it has, I will choose how to deal with it.

ACTIVITY 28: No blame

Think of three occasions when you were angry about something at work, and blamed individuals or institutional groups for the situation. In each case, replace your belief that it is someone else's fault with a belief that will reduce your anger rather than fuel it.

Blame belief	*No blame belief*
1	
2	
3	

The whole person

Seeing yourself or others entirely in terms of one or two negative characteristics leads to sustained anger and resentment and prevents healthy relationships and communication. Making yourself blind to the whole person by concentrating solely on the aspect of their personality that arouses your anger is unhelpful to everyone. It puts you in a state of constant annoyance as time and time again you see evidence of the behaviour that you dislike, and you feel more and more justified in your response. The other person, labelled and pinned down as untrustworthy or unreliable or whatever, is unable to form a positive relationship with you. If you choose to see the negative characteristic as just one part of the person, your anger will not be so readily triggered.

ACTIVITY 29: More than a label

Think of three situations in which your angry response is focused on one or two characteristics of a person. Describe the label you attach to the person, then think of a statement which helps you to focus on the whole person.

Labelling belief	*Accepting belief*
e.g. Sue is not a team player – she puts her personal agenda first.	Sue puts her agenda first. This does not mean that she is a bad person.
1	
2	
3	

Using rational self-talk

You can calm yourself down by giving yourself rational messages about the situation. When you want to cut short your angry emotional state, you can engage in a mental dialogue which allows a reasoned and positive view to take over as you talk yourself out of your hostile urges. For example, Tim in Scene 4 might want get into a calmer, more reasonable state before he decides how to deal with his problem with Gina. He could use a number of phrases designed to help him feel cooler: 'Keep calm. I am in control and I can handle this' or 'Relax. Don't let this get to you. Take it easy. I can manage this situation.' Stay-cool phrases you might use include:

I can hack this.
It's no big deal.
What's the worst thing that can happen here?
No-one can make me angry.
I won't shout.
I can get rid of my tension.
Slow down, take your time.
This will pass.
I can stay in control.
This is tough, but I can cope.
If this doesn't work I have other strategies.

ACTIVITY 30: Cool-down phrases

Choose two or three expressions that you could use as your stay-cool catch phrases. Think of a situation in which you would find it helpful to use this technique.

Situation	Words I could use	How I will feel
1		
2		
3		

Reframing

Reframing is an effective way of reducing and neutralizing angry and hostile feelings. What you do is put the person or the situation in an entirely different frame of reference from the one you usually apply. It is a different process from just looking for a positive or acceptable reason for someone's behaviour or for a justification of the facts of a situation – it is a way of taking the issue and looking at it from a new angle, as in the following example.

Scene 10: A different frame

Wesley is becoming very frustrated by some aspects of working in the public sector. He reacts angrily to the stream of initiatives and the constant changes to established practice. Since he cannot do anything to alter the situation and finds most areas of his work satisfying, he looks for a way of reframing the situation. He takes the view that he has an opportunity to develop his skills of working under pressure and adapting to new demands. This approach enables Wesley to diffuse his anger and irritation and to channel his energy in a constructive direction.

ACTIVITY 31: Reframing events

You may be able to reframe some of the events about which you become angry. Think about the frame of reference from which you assess events, then think of a completely different frame. A brainstorming approach may be helpful here – you are looking for creative ways to change your way of thinking!

Situation	Frame of reference	New frame of reference
1 Feeling annoyed about colleagues who put their personal life first	Behaviour at work	The importance and value of personal/ individual relationships

Situation	Frame of reference	New frame of reference
2		
3		
4		
5		
6		

Step into someone else's shoes

The ability to see things from someone else's point of view and to empathize with their feelings is an effective way to reduce your own anger and to build co-operative relationships. The art of empathy consists of understanding another person's world and being able to project yourself into their way of thinking. In a way it is a more powerful form of using rational self-talk, giving you insight into the other person's position and enabling you to experience the situation from a different perspective.

Practise becoming more aware of other people's feelings and motivation. Imaginative understanding of another person's point of view enables you to replace impatient and angry responses with more thoughtful and considered behaviour. Feeling empathy towards someone means that you step into the person's shoes and experience a situation as you imagine that person experiences it. You move outside your own frame of reference and understand the world as the other person sees it.

Do not confuse empathy with sympathy, although the two concepts are related. Being sympathetic involves offering support and approval, understanding and pity. Empathy operates outside the bounds of sympathy or approval. You can empathize with some-body, that is, put yourself in his or her place and see the world through that person's eyes, without actually feeling sympathetic. For example, you might not sympathize with a colleague who behaves in a way that you think is ruthless, but you may be able to feel empathy through an imaginative experience of the other's emotions, values and motivation.

Because the empathetic response offers non-judgemental understanding it is a powerful anger management tool, leading to increased tolerance and awareness of the differences between people. Empathy reduces cynicism and negativity and defuses hostile responses.

Scene 11: He's always getting at me

Rebecca feels that her line manager Neil is always on her case. Ever since he was promoted to this position, a month or so ago, he has constantly checked up on her work. Rebecca sees herself as competent and willing to take responsibility, and it irks her considerably that Neil delegates projects to her, then will not leave her alone to get on with them.

'It's not as if I'm inexperienced,' she complains to her friend. 'I'm perfectly capable of managing my own work, and I've never missed a deadline yet. It really gets me that he keeps checking up. I have to bite my tongue all the time in case I'm rude to him.'

'Perhaps it's because he's new to the job,' her friend suggests. 'He could be feeling under pressure not to make any mistakes, and that makes him anxious.'

Rebecca puts herself in Neil's position. She imagines the work situation as if she is Neil, seeing the new position and herself from Neil's point of view. She tries to experience what he is feeling, and she tunes in to his thoughts. Rebecca now feels empathy towards Neil, and no longer feels angry. She can make calm decisions about how to deal with the situation.

ACTIVITY 32: Apply empathy

When you have an automatic negative response towards someone, use your empathetic skill to alter your response by putting yourself in the other person's position. This exercise gives you some practice.

(a) Jot down the names of three people with whom you often feel angry or irritated. Visualize each person, including their behaviour and the way they speak. Visualize the settings in which your differences occur. How do you respond to this person?

FOUR-STEP PLAN FOR DEALING WITH ANGER

Source of conflict	Thoughts	Feelings	Behaviour
1			
2			
3			

(b) Now repeat the exercise from the other person's perspective. Imagine that you are the other person in each situation. How do you seem to that person? How does each person think and feel about you?

Source of conflict	Thoughts	Feelings	Behaviour
1			
2			
3			

Expressing your anger appropriately

Expressing your anger appropriately means saying the right words to the right person in the right way at the right time. Anger should be expressed in a way that acknowledges and respects other people's feelings and points of view, even if they conflict with our own. This may seem difficult enough to do in the best of circumstances, never mind in the demanding and sometimes stressful work environment. However, with thought, planning and careful handling, the expression of feelings can lead to positive and healthy relationships based on clear communication and understanding.

You need to think first of all about what outcome you want. The reason for expressing the way you feel might be to request a change in behaviour from the other person. If you are annoyed about something that you know cannot be changed, you may want to make clear that you are angry or dissatisfied even though you know that you have to accept the situation. Whatever the purpose that you identify, make sure that sharing your feelings is the best option.

Check that your anger is based on clear, not distorted thinking, and that to express it is worthwhile because the situation is important enough to you to be dealt with in this way.

Whatever the individual circumstances, there are some outcomes that are to be desired whenever you tell someone how angry you are. In the first place, let us assume that you want to keep your job. We are not discussing here the kind of expression of dissatisfaction that is the prelude to handing in your notice, or the kind of uncontrolled outburst that might lead to you losing your job: we are looking at situations which spark your anger and which need to be managed carefully in order to maintain and improve working relationships. The most important outcome is that both you and the other person maintain respect for yourselves and for each other.

Once you have checked who you are angry with, and what exactly you are angry about, plan how you will communicate your feelings.

The right words

The most important word in this kind of assertive communication is 'I'. You are acknowledging and owning your feelings, not blaming the other person for making you angry. Remember, no-one can make you angry. Use words like 'I feel', 'I get angry'. Don't say 'You make me so angry', 'The trouble with you is . . .', 'Why can't you . . .?' Also avoid using neutral, third-person phrases such as 'It makes me mad' and 'This kind of situation is annoying.' Don't distance yourself from the feeling – it is yours and you are responsible for it.

Get the right word or words to describe precisely the level of anger that you feel. (Look back at Activity 18 for some suggestions about this.) Decide if you feel enraged, or slightly irritated, furious or a bit put out. Rehearse exactly what you want to say. It is a good idea to begin by setting the scene with something like, 'There's something I want to say about yesterday's meeting.' Be straightforward and direct about your feelings: 'I'm feeling very annoyed.' If you feel awkward or embarrassed or even scared that the person will think worse of you, or sack you, there is no harm in saying so. If part of the awkwardness or embarrassment is because you have a good working relationship with the person, say so. 'I don't like saying this, because we usually work so well together.' Go on to describe the behaviour that has triggered your response. Again, make it very specific. Phrases such as 'I didn't like the way you acted' are too vague to be helpful. Find the right words to identify the problem or issue so that your meaning is clear and not open to different interpretations. For example, you might say, 'You interrupted me twice when I was presenting my proposal' or 'You tapped your fingers and fidgeted all the time I was explaining my idea.' The other person is responsible for their behaviour; you are responsible for your response. Do not use any words that blame or label the person you are speaking to, and do not refer to previous incidents. Stick to the issue at hand. Finish by saying what you want to happen. It might be something like, 'Please don't behave like that at next week's meeting' or 'I'm asking you in future not to interrupt during my presentation. There is time for comments and discussion afterwards.'

If the response is along the lines of 'I didn't do that – you must be imagining it' or 'I don't know what you're so upset about', stay calm, and just repeat what you have already said. Acknowledge the response – 'You might think that you did not behave in that way, but I'm telling you what I observed' or 'Well, I'll tell you again what I am upset about.' Do not allow yourself to be deflected or drawn into argument or an attack on the other person. Stay focused on the purpose of what you are saying.

The right way

How you say the words that you have chosen is a very important part of your message. Your body language and tone of voice should support the idea of calm and legitimate assertion of your feelings. Make your posture relaxed and upright, and keep your hand and body movements open. Don't cover your face with your hands, or clasp your arms across your chest. Stand or sit at a comfortable distance from the other person, not so far away that you seem nervous, and not so close that they feel crowded or threatened. Keep steady eye contact, and make your facial expression responsive but not smiling. Make your voice firm and steady and speak in a reasonably loud tone to be easily heard. Avoid sounding sarcastic, or whining, or jocular. Don't sound over-forceful, or apologetic, and don't detract from what you are saying by fiddling with your hair or fingers or items such as pens and papers.

The right place and time

You should speak to the person in private. An audience of any kind brings another dimension into play, and may make either or both of you feel self-conscious. Although your behaviour is based on respect for yourself and the other person, and will in no way diminish or belittle him or her, it is important to give the other person the opportunity to maintain control. Allowing somebody an escape route and ensuring that they are in a face-saving position is empathetic and considerate, and will underline the appropriateness of your communication. Timing can play a significant role here. You need to demonstrate that once you have expressed your feelings, the matter is closed (unless, of course, you need to re-address the subject at a later date) and to show by your behaviour immediately afterwards that usual relationships are resumed. For this reason, you might consider timing this encounter for a point during the day such as just before a lunch or coffee break, which gives a natural breaking point and enables you to interact with the person shortly afterwards.

Planning and rehearsing will give you the confidence to express your anger appropriately. Managing your emotions effectively and communicating your feelings in this way will help to turn negative situations into positive opportunities for increased understanding and co-operation.

ACTIVITY 33: Appropriate expression

Think of a situation in which it will be appropriate to express your feelings of anger. Plan how you will do this.

Situation _____

Who I will speak to _____

Where and when _____

The words I will use _____

How I will speak _____

What gestures I will use _____

What my body will feel like _____

What emotions I will feel _____

How I will feel afterwards _____

4

Dealing with Triggers

Recognizing your flash points

If you know what triggers your anger you can take steps to stop your angry response. In Chapter 1 we looked at the kinds of situation that make us angry and how our physical, emotional and mental responses are activated when we perceive threats to our well-being. Although there are general principles which apply to how everyone experiences anger and hostility, it is important for you to be aware of your personal triggers and how they affect you. You will then have the choice of:

(a) avoiding the trigger;
(b) defusing the situation;
(c) changing the way you think about the trigger.

Know your triggers

Particular events, situations and people will trigger your anger response. The triggers will be things that you perceive as threats. At work, feelings of frustration, annoyance, anger are aroused by the kind of situation that you have identified as you worked through the previous chapters. Think more closely now about what sparks off your angry feelings. Although reactions will vary, there are some situations which tend to trigger angry reactions in the work environment on a widespread basis. These include:

co-workers and bosses who do not pull their weight
not being listened to
being blamed and criticized unfairly
put-down remarks
refusal to take responsibility
lack of praise
gossip and rumours
not being promoted
heavy or unrealistic workload
unrealistic deadlines
managers playing favourites
others' incompetence

misuse of authority
lack of training

Do any of these hit a nerve with you? Think now about the precise circumstances in which you experience the trigger. After all, not many of us sit at work getting into an angry state thinking generally about frustrating or annoying situations. (If you do find yourself getting angry as thoughts and memories keep surfacing and running through your head, try the thought-stopping and distraction techniques described later.) It is more likely that in the course of a working day we encounter something which provokes our anger. It may be a conversation, the sight of someone or something, an email, a phone call, a demand, a request, a joke. Our reaction may vary according to the time of day, or the particular environment or circumstances.

ACTIVITY 34: Your triggers

(a) In the chart below, write three occasions on which your anger response was triggered. Be as precise as you can in identifying the nature of the trigger. The last column is for you to describe the level of anger that was triggered in each case.

Trigger (specify person/event)	*Place*	*Time*	*High*	*Medium*	*Low*
1 _____			☐	☐	☐
2 _____			☐	☐	☐
3 _____			☐	☐	☐

(b) Keep a log of your anger triggers over a period of at least a week.

Tune in to your body

Start to recognize the warning signs that you are becoming worked up about something. Your body's instinctive reaction will alert you. The earlier you realize that something has lit your fuse, the sooner you can take steps to remain calm and stop yourself getting fired up.

ACTIVITY 35: Physical signals

Which of the following symptoms signal your anger response? Check the ones that you usually experience:

faster heartbeat
faster breathing
dry mouth
clenched hands
sweaty palms
louder voice
faster movements
feelings of panic
going red in the face
feeling twitchy and fidgety

Any other symptoms:

How to handle your triggers

Once you are familiar with the triggers that provoke your anger or irritation, decide what you are going to do in order to stop yourself getting more heated.

Avoid the trigger

It may be possible to avoid situations and people that get to you. There are two ways of looking at this: you can literally avoid them by keeping a physical distance between you, or you can prevent the trigger situation by changing your behaviour.

Scene 12: Karina's coffee breaks

Karina has her morning coffee break with the same group of colleagues every day. At first she enjoyed the chat and the gossip about their fellow workers, but recently Karina has become very irritated with what she sees as their tendency to moan and complain all the time. Instead of being a relaxing break, she finds that these occasions leave her feeling tetchy and grumpy. Her heart sinks as she makes her way to the coffee machine, and she feels slightly worked up already, just anticipating how the conversation will go and how she will feel at the end of it.

The coffee break is a trigger for Karina's anger. Once she recognizes and acknowledges her response, she can choose to defuse her anger by using an appropriate calming strategy or by seeing the situation differently. However, having checked out the basis and validity of her thoughts, and having decided that she does not want to express her feelings to the group, Karina chooses to avoid the trigger. She does not need to take her break with this group of people, and she decides to use the time in a way that will leave her feeling positive and energized instead of irritable and out of sorts.

Change your behaviour

When it is not possible to avoid the situation or the individual which acts as a trigger for your anger, you could see if there are any ways in which you could change your behaviour in order to disrupt the trigger–response pattern. Your usual reaction in the situation may be valid and reasonable, and you may feel that there is no reason why you should behave any differently. However, if the situation inevitably arouses angry feelings, you might consider taking steps to make things less heated.

Scene 13: Greg cuts it fine

Greg puts together the figures he has collated for the meeting later that week, and sends them over for Vik to look at. As he does so he knows how Vik will react, and feel himself becoming irritated just thinking about it.

Sure enough, Vik sends him an email. 'Got the figures. I'll try to look at them before the meeting, but you're cutting it fine as usual.'

Greg then becomes very irritated. He is within the agreed deadline for submitting the figures, and doesn't see why he should put up with Vik's comments. This is what happens every month. Greg passes over the figures just in time, and Vik gives a response that triggers Greg's annoyance.

Greg could choose to deal with this situation by changing his behaviour. It is possible for him to get the figures in earlier – he has just become used to doing this task at the last minute. Although he is doing nothing wrong, in that he is not late in submitting the account, he decides that next month he will do the work at the earliest rather than the latest time. This means that he will prevent the trigger situation. Vik will not feel the need to give his usual response, and Greg will not become angry.

ACTIVITY 36: Trigger avoidance

Think about situations in which you could remain calm either by physically avoiding what triggers your anger, or by changing your behaviour so that the trigger is not set off.

Trigger situation   How I can avoid /disrupt the trigger–response pattern

1 _____

2 _____

3 _____

Be an actor

You could try behaving or acting your way into feeling calm and in control. Behaving as if you are experiencing a certain emotional state can result in your actually generating that state. If you act calmly, you will feel calm. Try playing the part of a person who is not easily angered – if you like, you could identify someone you know whose responses are calm and controlled and model your behaviour on theirs. Practise physical actions that are the opposite of those that indicate an angry response. Relax your muscles, keep your hands open instead of clenched, breathe slowly and deeply. See yourself behaving like someone who is in control. Reinforce your physical behaviour with rational, calming statements to yourself. You will find that even if you feel wound up inside, behaving as if you are not at all tense will calm you down and will prevent your automatic trigger response.

Give yourself a certain length of time for behaving in a non-angry way, a few days, perhaps, or a week. Notice the differences in how you feel and in how others respond towards you.

Keeping your cool

If you are patient in one moment of anger, you will escape a hundred days of sorrow.

Chinese proverb

Sometimes it is not possible to avoid what triggers your anger, and sometimes our angry response can take us by surprise. You may have been in situations in which you thought you were calm, until someone or something hits a button and you feel yourself beginning to flare up. Now and again you may need to reinforce the strategies that you have put in place. The following suggestions offer ways of stopping yourself becoming more angry.

Relax

It is actually difficult to feel angry if your body is relaxed! When you experience the early warning signs of anger, use some of the calming phrases described in Chapter 3, and at the same time try consciously to relax the muscles which have tensed up. Focus on those muscles which signal your anger response, probably your neck and shoulder muscles, or your back and spine. Feel the tension in each muscle group, then in turn release each one so that you feel the tension draining away.

Breathing properly also helps you to remain calm. Breathe in slowly and deeply, feeling your abdomen expand as you do so, hold your breath for five seconds, then breathe out slowly, expelling all the air in your lungs. Do this several times, keeping every breath slow, steady and measured. You will feel yourself becoming calmer.

Thought-stopping

Use this technique when you want to get rid of hostile thoughts and urges that persist in your mind in spite of your attempts to talk yourself down. What you do is quite literally stop the thought. You could mentally (or physically if you are alone!) yell the word 'Stop!' You could reinforce this by clapping your hands loudly. It might work to associate the thoughts with something painful, like a pinch, or digging your nails into your palm, something that you can do when you have these thoughts and want to get rid of them. Another method you could try is visualization. Imagine your angry thoughts rolled up into a tight little ball, and hit the ball as far as you can away from yourself. Watch it fly off and disappear over the horizon.

Distraction

When you feel yourself getting angry and there is no appropriate way to change the situation, try to distract yourself from your emotional state. Find something else to focus on. It could be something physical, such as a picture or other object in the room. If there are documents, files, magazines around, choose to concentrate on one of them. Even a crack in the ceiling will do – you just need something else to think about to give the angry thoughts less of a chance to get a hold.

You could try playing the kind of game that is often used to distract children on a car journey. Think of the name of an animal beginning with each letter of the alphabet, or try counting backwards from one hundred, or reciting a song or a poem. The nature of the activity does not matter, as long as it is sufficiently absorbing to distract you from your anger.

ACTIVITY 37: Stop angry thoughts

Practise shouting 'Stop!' Go over in your mind the kinds of thoughts and emotions you experience when you are becoming angry. Cut short your train of thought by saying 'Stop!' very loudly and firmly.

ACTIVITY 38: Focus on something else

Think of three situations at work in which you could use the distraction technique to stop your hostile or angry thoughts.

Situation   Distraction technique I could use

1 _____

2 _____

3 _____

Take time out

Sometimes you may need to remove yourself from a situation in order to calm down or remain calm. It might be possible to leave the room you are in and to deflect your angry feelings by cooling down. You could go for a short walk, or practise some of the relaxation techniques describe earlier. It might be possible to listen to some music which you know has a calming effect on you, or you could try visualizing yourself in a tranquil setting, on a beach, perhaps, or doing something restful and enjoyable. If you do walk away in order to get into a calmer frame of mind and body, do not do anything while you are away to inflame your feelings or stimulate them further. Do not phone someone to let off steam; do not go over and over what has been said. At this point, it is best not to make any decisions about how to handle the situation. Leave dealing with the problem until you feel confident that you can cope without losing your cool.

Of course, there are some situations you cannot physically leave. You might be in a conference with a client, or in a staff meeting where leaving the room may draw unwelcome attention your way. What you can do is take a mental time-out by employing some of the methods of distraction and calming self-talk that are described above. When you take a mental time-out it is particularly effective to focus on an image that you associate with calm and tranquillity, such as a natural scene that invokes feelings of peace and well-being. Find one that works for you. It might be a beach, or a favourite country walk, or a wood, or a waterfall. Make it clear and vibrant in your mind, and practise creating the image so that you can call it up whenever you want to become calm. There are some more ideas about this in Chapter 7.

See the funny side

Humour is a powerful way of reducing anger and hostility. Try to laugh at yourself by seeing the funny side of your reactions. When you find yourself getting worked up, mentally exaggerate the situation so that you seem ridiculous – turn yourself into a dragon breathing fire over a comparatively trivial event, or laugh at your self-importance for expecting the world to turn the way that suits you. Focus only on the aspect of your behaviour that is fuelling your anger – don't put yourself down by becoming your own laughing stock! You could try this with other people as well, but be careful not to use humour as a form of aggression. This will only fuel your hostility. Keep it light and funny. You could imagine the person with whom you are angry as a cartoon character, or as a baby, or you could mentally dress him or her in an outrageous outfit. Again, make fun only of the aspect of the person that is contributing to your anger. Laughter is a positive emotion, which can lift you out of a tense and hostile frame of mind. Make sure that you use it for a positive result.

Put up the shield

Try this way of preventing the trigger from affecting you. Imagine that there is a strong invisible shield between you and the person or situation. The shield will protect you from words and actions, and you will not respond to any provocation. Nothing that is done or said can affect you. Behind your shield, you can remain calm and objective and decide how to deal with the situation. Once the crisis is over, mentally put your shield away until you want to use it again.

Change the way you think about the trigger

Step Four of the Four-Step Plan outlined in Chapter 3 suggests a number of ways of changing how you think about a person or situation. If you make a conscious effort to challenge old thoughts and rigid beliefs about yourself, other people and the world in general, you will be more able to alter your perception of the things that provoke your anger.

ACTIVITY 39: Make a plan

Take time now to draw up your own MAP – Managing Anger Plan. Start by identifying the circumstances that are likely to trigger your anger, and for each one MAP out how you will deal with your thoughts and feelings.

Likely trigger _____

Signs that tell me I'm getting angry _____

How I can keep calm _____

Coping statement I can use _____

My thoughts about the trigger _____

What I will do _____

5

Dealing with Angry People

Facing someone's anger can be a distressing and even frightening experience. How you deal with the situation depends on a number of factors, such as the level of the person's anger, how it is expressed and where it is expressed. As you know, anger is not always revealed in overtly aggressive or threatening language and behaviour. A colleague may express hostile feelings by using sarcasm or verbal put-downs, or by undermining your work or your position. There may be a temptation to ignore or avoid such indirect expressions of anger, but if you make this choice, check that your decision is based on clear thinking and not on fear or intimidation. What you cannot ignore or avoid is the kind of angry outburst directed at you which takes you by surprise, and unless managed carefully, can result in your becoming angry in return and making the situation worse.

The unexpected explosion

First of all, remember that you are responsible for your own feelings. You are not responsible for someone else's emotional state. However, your response to another's emotional state affects the way it develops, and when someone is angry, your behaviour can add fuel to the flames, or it can take the heat out of the situation. Apply what you have learnt about your own experience of anger to help you deal with someone who is in the grip of hostile emotions. You know that at this point the person will not be rational, will not have good judgement and will not be in control. You must control your own internal and external responses in order to bring about the outcome you want, which is to defuse the situation and bring the person to a calmer frame of mind. Only at that point will you be able to address the issue that is bothering them. Your priority when facing someone's angry eruption is not to respond to what they are angry about, but to get to a position where you can have a reasonable discussion.

Keep calm

Act immediately to short-circuit your own instinctive response to a threat. Control your physical response and prevent your body from going into 'fight or flight' mode. Make your body calm and relaxed by employing the breathing techniques we looked at earlier. Breathe deeply at a regular pace – your brain needs oxygen to help you think, and in this situation you need to be able to think clearly. Really, you need to think for two. The person you are dealing with cannot think clearly; when we are in an angry state, reason and judgement are suspended. Make a conscious effort to relax your muscles.

Control your thoughts by repeating to yourself a coping statement such as the ones described in Chapter 3. You could say to yourself something like, 'This is a tough situation, but I can deal with it', or 'I am not responsible for this person's feelings, and I cannot change this person.' Don't take what is being said personally, even if you are the subject of a verbal attack. Try the shield technique described earlier – imagine the words flying towards you but not hitting their target. Imagine them remaining in the air, suspended, harmless. The person's judgement is poor at this point. What is being said may not be what is meant. Later, you will sort that out. In the meantime, you have a range of coping strategies to help you deal with this situation.

Of course it is difficult to remain completely calm, and you would not wish to be inappropriately relaxed, or give the impression of being passive. You need to feel and seem alert and focused. Controlling your responses will help you to behave rationally rather than emotionally.

Control your body language
Be aware of your body language when you are dealing with an angry person. You should appear non-threatening. Try to get yourself on the same physical level – towering above someone could seem aggressive, and remaining at a lower level could feel threatening to you. Keep a comfortable space between you. Move so that you are sideways on to each other rather than face to face, a position that can seem confrontational. Be careful not to move towards the other person, as an invasion of space can seem threatening. Do not put yourself between the person and the exit. This might cause the person to feel trapped, and it makes you put yourself in the role of an obstacle or hurdle that has to be overcome. At the same time, do not let him or her get between you and an exit. You should both feel that you have the same access to a way out of the room or space.

Check to see if your hands have gone into fists. Let them hang loosely by your side, or use open-palm gestures and gradually slowing movements to communicate a feeling of growing calm. Try not to make uncontrolled, excitable gestures which may stimulate the other person further, and do not touch him or her. Monitor your eye contact. Be careful not to get locked into a stare or prolonged gaze.

You may want to move out of the space you are in. The eruption might have occurred in public, in which case you may want to protect co-workers (or even customers or clients) from the incident. If it happens in private, in an enclosed office, for example, you may feel more comfortable in a more open environment. Encourage movement to a safer space by walking in the direction of the place you want to be, talking as you go.

Choose your words

What you say at this stage is very important. There may be a lot of things you want to say. You might feel that the person has got it all wrong and is saying things that are not true, but this is not the time to say anything about the issues involved. In fact, the less said the better. What you need to do is acknowledge the person's feelings. 'I can see that you are angry' might seem a rather lame response to a forceful outburst, but these or similar words expressed in a calm, level tone help to bring down the temperature. You are not ignoring the person's feelings, nor are you saying that the feelings are irrational or inappropriate. Find a form of words that is suitable for the person and the situation. 'I can see this has really got to you.' 'Okay, John, I can see you're really distressed.' Be careful not to sound sarcastic or condescending. It is a good idea to use the person's name. This gets their attention and enables you to proceed with the calming-down process.

There are some phrases you should definitely *not* use.

Calm down.
I don't know what you're getting so het up about.
There's no need to get so angry.

The tone and pitch of your voice can help to reduce the other person's level of arousal. Sounding excessively calm and low-key in response to someone who is speaking forcefully and agitatedly can in fact be inflammatory, but at the same time you do not want to speak as loudly and intensely as the other. It is better at first to speak at just a level or two beneath the other person's, then gradually lower your voice.

Reveal your own feelings

You could let the other person know how you feel, but without blaming them for your response. This will reduce the tension and help you to maintain control. Saying, 'I feel nervous when you speak so loudly' or 'I'm feeling quite disturbed at the moment, and can't think straight. We should discuss this later' are ways of making the other person aware of their behaviour and its effect in a fairly neutral way.

Be alert

If at any point you feel uncomfortable or even in danger when, for example, someone is shouting at you or showing signs of becoming physically aggressive, you can just walk away. You may explain your action: 'John, I'm walking away because you are shouting at me.' You may wish to specify the consequences of certain behaviour: 'John, I will not listen to you for another minute if you continue to bang on the table.'

Do not hesitate to ask for help if you judge it to be necessary. You needn't be dramatic about this, but you could say something like, 'I'm going to ask Jane to come in on this one.'

Take it on board

Show that you are willing to listen. Make it clear that you want to address the problem and find a solution. Show that you will deal with the matter constructively. However, this is not the time to resolve the crisis. You must wait until the other person is calm enough to respond rationally. This could be in ten minutes' time, it could mean waiting a day. Agree a time and a place to discuss whatever it was that caused such an angry reaction.

Scene 14: Stuart's outburst

Do you remember Stuart and Geraldine from Scene 2? Stuart has planned a special evening and is looking forward to going home early. Geraldine is approaching him with a request.

'Stuart, I'd like you stay on for a bit and put in this extra data,' she says. Stuart usually agrees to last-minute requests and always does a good job. Hardly waiting for an answer, she puts the file on the desk and nods her thanks. To her surprise, Stuart bangs the desk with his fist so hard that the file falls off.

'I've had enough of this!' he explodes. 'I'm sick and tired of being taken for granted!' His voice is loud and insistent, and he is getting red in the face. Geraldine backs away, a little frightened by the force of his feelings. Her heart is thumping uncomfortably and she begins to tremble.

Stuart gets up from his desk and pushes his chair to one side. 'That's the trouble with this place – one or two people do most of the work, and they end up being dumped on all the time. Well, I'm not going to put up with it any more!' He is shouting now, and on the other side of the room people are looking up from their computer screens. Oblivious of their stares, Stuart starts to fling his possessions in his bag. Geraldine shakily says, 'Calm down, Stuart.' This makes things worse. 'Don't you tell me to calm down!' he says. 'It's people like you who create this situation in the first place!'

ACTIVITY 40: Managing the outburst

What would be an effective way for Geraldine to handle Stuart's angry outburst? Make notes under the following headings.

What is the first thing Geraldine should do? _____

What self-calming techniques could Geraldine use? _____

What could Geraldine say? _____

How should she say it? _____

What should Geraldine do? _____

How should she do it? _____

How Stuart might react _____

What the outcome might be _____

Now think of an unexpected outburst of anger that you have experienced, and decide how you will deal with a similar situation in the future.

Situation _____

How I will stay calm _____

What I will say _____

How I will say it _____

What I will do _____

How I will do it _____

What the outcome may be _____

_____

Preventing an angry explosion

If you intervene quickly and appropriately you can prevent someone's anger from reaching boiling point. Look out for the warning signs of anger or frustration. You may notice signs such as:

> breathing more quickly
> going red in the face
> speaking more loudly or quickly than usual
> clenching their fists or hunching their shoulders
> hands shaking
> fidgety actions

As well as these physical signs, you might notice aspects of behaviour:

> muttering and complaining
> sarcasm
> personal attacks
> standard of work slipping
> taking longer breaks
> becoming less punctual
> too quiet atmosphere
> clock watching
> over-politeness

When you sense that there is an angry storm brewing, take the initiative to stop it building up. You are not angry, you are in control of your actions and emotions, and your behaviour can help the angry person to calm down. Angry people are not in control of their emotions and their judgement is poor. It is essential that you remain calm and that you do not meet anger with anger – that will only cause the situation to become more heated and out of control.

Scene 15: Storm averted

Meera is on the phone to one of their clients when Nancy rushes in. 'Have you got the layouts for the new brochure? I need them for my meeting with Brown Lacey.'

Meera mimes that she has not got the layouts and continues her conversation. Nancy comes closer. 'But you must have them!' She sounds agitated. 'I gave them to you to check yesterday!' She rummages through the papers on Meera's desk. 'The trouble with you is that you just can't keep up to date with things. We'll lose the account if they think that we're behind with the schedule!'

Meera realizes that Nancy is becoming angry and agitated. She says to her caller, 'Something has just come up. I'll ring you back shortly.'

Rule 1: Be calm

Meera applies Rule 1. She makes sure that her breathing is slow and steady, and she makes conscious movements to relax her body and her muscles. As well as paying attention to her physical state, Meera takes control of her mental responses. She tells herself not to take what Nancy is saying personally. Nancy is getting into an angry emotional state and her comments and judgement may not be entirely valid. Meera repeats a coping statement to herself: 'I can deal with this. I can handle this situation.'

Rule 2: Focus on the issue

The first issue to be dealt with is the presenting problem – the need to have something to show the client. Meera takes some of the heat out of the situation by focusing on how to deal with the problem. She does not respond to Nancy's comment that she cannot keep up to date with the work, and she does not respond to Nancy's anger. In this case Meera knows that she is not responsible for what has gone wrong, but she chooses not to dwell on who is to blame or how the misunderstanding could have occurred. Instead she says, 'You really didn't give the layouts to me yesterday, but the important thing right now is to make sure that you have a copy of them for the meeting. What can I do to help?'

The second thing to do is to address the underlying problem. The real issue at stake could be a number of things. It could be anxiety about dealing with this particular client; it could be that the company is taking on more work than it can handle; it could be that they accept unrealistic deadlines; it could be that they have unclear procedures and working practices. Because Nancy's anger is not at boiling point, it is possible for Meera to engage in a conversation focused on what might be the problem. A very angry person is not able to respond rationally, and so there is no point in trying to have a discussion. If, however, you gauge that, as here, the anger is growing but has not reached the point of explosion, it is a good idea to move quickly to prevent hostility from escalating. When Meera and Nancy have found a way of dealing with the immediate problem, Meera moves on the discussion by saying, 'I can see that you were very agitated about not being prepared for the meeting with Brown Lacey.' She opens the way for Nancy to talk about how she feels and for them both to look at problems that they are experiencing.

Rule 3: Listen

Listening to what the other person has to say is crucial. Only by hearing and understanding what they are thinking and feeling is it possible to move forward to a solution and restore the equilibrium. There are four behavioural modes of listening:

(a) listening;
(b) responding;
(c) asking questions;
(d) keeping quiet.

In order to listen attentively, you need to focus exclusively on the other person. For the time being Meera has to forget about the phone call she was making and the pile of work on her desk. She lets Nancy know that she is listening by her body language. Meera's relaxed body posture, appropriate facial expressions, good eye contact and encouraging nods communicate interest and attention.

The most effective way of responding in this situation is to feed back to the speaker the essence of what they are saying. This does not mean that you repeat parrot-fashion what has been said, but that you offer a summary or paraphrase that shows you have understood both the facts and the emotions that have been expressed. As Nancy expresses some of her anger and frustration, Meera says things like, 'So you feel very wound up and worried that we might lose this account.' The knowledge that she is being listened to and that attention is being paid to her feelings stops Nancy from becoming more angry.

There are some forms of responding that are to be avoided. Do not blame or attack the other person, and do not judge or evaluate what is being said. It is also not a good idea to jump in with advice or suggestions – particularly not with suggestions about how people should deal with their anger. Remember that you are focusing on issues, not behaviour. Expressions such as 'You're wrong about that' or 'You don't understand' will have the opposite of the effect you want and will only add fuel to the person's anger. Instead, use understanding phrases such as 'I can see how it may seem that way to you.'

The right questions will help the angry person to explain and explore their feelings, and will give you the information you need to be able to understand. Open questions will encourage someone to communicate. 'What do you think about . . . ?'; 'Tell me about . . .' are questions that prompt descriptive responses. Hypothetical questions such as 'What if we . . . ?' or 'Suppose that . . .' are useful ways in to finding solutions. When you are in the process of defusing someone's anger, try not to ask 'Why?' If Meera asked, 'Why didn't you make sure that I saw the layouts well in advance of the meeting?' Nancy would probably feel attacked, and would leap to defend herself. Meera asks, 'What prevented you from getting the layouts to me earlier?' This form of question allows Nancy to express her frustration at her heavy workload and lack of adequate assistance without feeling threatened or put on the spot.

Use silence to allow time for both parties to take in what the other is saying. Resist the temptation to jump in and answer your own questions. If the silence indicates that the person cannot answer the question or respond to the suggestion, then try asking it in a different way.

Listen for what the person's needs are. This means that you have to pay attention to more than just the words and their surface meaning. As you know, anger can spring from unfulfilled needs and desires. It is possible that the angry person needs attention, or reassurance, or any of the needs that are discussed in Chapter 1. Aggression is sometimes a way of covering up insecurity. Focusing on the person's needs and motives is a form of self-protection as well as a crucial step to understanding, and will help you to manage your own emotional response.

Rule 4: Decide on some action

These strategies have helped to prevent the build-up of anger. Bring the encounter to a positive conclusion by agreeing on some action – even if no definite outcome has emerged and your agreement is to meet again to discuss the matter. In this case, Meera and Nancy agree that they will need to take on some administrative help if their company is to keep its existing commitments and continue to grow.

ACTIVITY 41: Dealing with an angry person

Think about an occasion when you feel that you did not deal effectively with someone who is angry. Decide how you might handle the situation in a different way. Write your comments here.

What was not effective in my behaviour   *How I would behave differently*

1 _____

2 _____

3 _____

4 _____

Dealing with indirect anger

Anger expressed indirectly can be tricky to handle. Because the shows of hostility are subtle and veiled they may be ignored or tolerated. This situation will lead to hidden tensions and resentments, which may well erupt in an angry outburst one day when the behaviour flicks the recipient on the raw. If you think that someone is masking aggression through the use of sarcasm and jokes, for example, it is a good idea to confront the problem before the situation becomes worse. You do have the choice to ignore this behaviour, but before you decide which way to handle it, ask yourself some questions:

How much does this negative behaviour bother me?
Am I contributing to this negative behaviour?
What do I gain by ignoring it?

What do I gain by dealing with it?
Have I got the skills to deal with it? (ability to manage mental and physical responses; verbal and non-verbal skills)

If the behaviour bothers you, and if by dealing with it you will gain self-respect and a more understanding relationship with your co-worker, then you should bring the issue into the open.

Sarcasm and put-downs

Respond to a sarcastic comment or a put-down by treating it at face value. Rather than argue with what has been said, ask for more information. Asking the speaker to clarify what is meant is a way of distinguishing between seriously meant criticisms and manipulative put-downs. 'What do you mean by that?' If the comment contains some truth, acknowledge what is true and reject the rest. 'I know I was late back from lunch once or twice recently, but I don't think that justifies calling me the Late Luncher of the Year.' If the criticism is not true, reject it. 'I disagree with that description of my behaviour.' If you want only to keep at a distance from the comment while still showing that you will not simply ignore it, just agree that, from the other person's perspective, there might be some truth in what was said: 'I can see that it might seem that way.'

Scene 16: Yes-woman

Jacqui says to Lee, 'I have to agree with Kevin. I think we should change the structure of the monthly meetings in order to make better use of the time available.'

Helen shrugs and says, 'Well, I think that all we need to do is make sure that the meetings are chaired effectively.' She turns away and adds under her voice, 'But there's no point in arguing with Sanjay's yes-woman.'

Jacqui hears the comment, which is not the first of its kind that Helen has made. She knows that it is time to deal with the situation. The first thing she does is check her physical and mental responses so that she does not counter-attack. She breathes slowly and steadily, and relaxes her neck and shoulders. Then, in a calm, level voice she asks Helen to clarify what she has said.

'I'm wondering what you mean, Helen, by calling me Sanjay's yes-woman. Could you explain?'

Helen looks startled, and rather embarrassed. 'Well, nothing really. It's just that you always seem to agree with him.'

Jacqui thinks about this. 'I do often agree with him, but not always, and not automatically. What have I said or done to make you think that I just say yes to whatever Sanjay says?'

Helen says, 'Nothing really. I was just being funny.'

'Well, I want to let you know that I don't find that kind of comment very amusing.'

Jacqui has dealt effectively with Helen's put-down. She does not know what the source of Helen's hostility is, and she realizes that it may be nothing at all to do with her. Jacqui can choose now whether to explore the issue further. She could round off the discussion with Helen by saying something like, 'I'm glad we've cleared that up' and go on to encourage her to say what is really annoying her.

ACTIVITY 42: Put-downs

What responses could you make to these put-downs? The first one has been done for you.

Put-down	*Response*
You really don't like change, do you?	I don't see it that way. What do you mean?
That's typical of you.	_____
Don't worry about it.	_____
You don't really believe that, do you?	_____
If I were you . . .	_____
You must have plenty of time.	_____

Offensive remarks

You may want to deal with other kinds of hostile comments in which the offensive factor is sometimes masked by a show of humour. This is often the case with sexist, racist or homophobic remarks, or indeed any behaviour which discriminates against or mocks a particular section of society.

Scene 17: Not so funny

Jim is becoming increasingly annoyed by his colleague Brett's jokes about people of the older generation. He has tried to respond to Brett's quips with humour, but the jokes continue, and the atmosphere in the office is becoming tense. Jim decides to speak to Brett privately. First of all, he reveals his feelings about the issue.

'Brett, I want to tell you that I don't like it when you make fun of older people on account of their age.' Jim goes on to say how the behaviour affects others in the workplace. 'I've noticed that other people are uncomfortable when you joke like that.'

Brett says, 'I'm only having a bit of a joke. What's the problem, are you too old to have a sense of humour?'

Jim remains calm. (Think about the kind of self-calming strategies he might use at this point.) He keeps his voice steady and maintains eye contact with Brett. 'My sense of humour is fine – your jokes about older people aren't funny. Please stop making them.'

Brett shrugs and says, 'I don't understand why you're making such a fuss.'

Jim does not get drawn into a discussion about his attitude. He acknowledges what Brett has said, and repeats the message. 'I realize that you do not understand my feelings on this matter, but I find your jokes inappropriate, and I would like you to stop making them.'

Spreading rumours or gossip

How you deal with this will depend on whether you are present when the behaviour occurs, or if someone tells you about it, as might be the case if you yourself are the subject of conversation. If you ascertain that someone is talking about you, tackle the person directly. Many people deny rumour-spreading or gossip-mongering. Do not get into an argument about the facts of the behaviour, but focus on dealing effectively with the hidden aggression it suggests.

Scene 18: Harmful gossip

Laura knows that Sophie has been gossiping behind her back. She says to Sophie, 'Can we talk for a few minutes? There's something I'd like to discuss.' When she has Sophie's attention, Laura says, 'I'm feeling a little disturbed about the things that you have been saying about me. It's been brought to my attention by a few people that you have been talking about what I did on the residential course last month. What bothers me is that you felt the need to behave in this way.'

'I don't know who's told you that!' Sophie blusters. 'They've got it all wrong!'

'I'm glad to hear that. If it were true, it would be something we need to discuss. I'd particularly want to talk about anything in our working relationship which might have caused this situation.'

Being cold and unfriendly

If someone is giving you the cold shoulder, show that you have noticed the behaviour and would like to discuss it. Open the subject by describing precisely what behaviour you have observed. Comments like 'You're not very friendly towards me' are too vague and can be side-stepped. Be direct and specific. 'Are you annoyed with me? I have noticed that you don't stop to chat any more, and you avoid me at lunch time.' Remember that you are trying to find out if the person is feeling angry and hostile towards you. If you have given offence or cause for annoyance, and the person takes advantage of this opportunity to tell you about it, listen to the criticism calmly and respond with the same kind of assertion with which you handle sarcasm and put-downs. 'I can see that I behaved thoughtlessly when I spent a lot of time talking to David when the three of us had lunch. Thanks for pointing it out. I hope this will clear the air, and we can pick up where we left off.'

ACTIVITY 43: Indirect anger

Decide how you would deal with these expressions of indirect anger.

Example	*What I would do*	*What I would say*
1 Someone who sabotages your work		
2 Someone who embarrasses you at a meeting		

Your example:

3 _____

6

Turning Conflict into Co-operation

Conflict at work is inevitable. The differences which make us unique
– our individual personalities, values, ideas – are sources of potential
conflict. In general, normal instincts of self-interest combined with
normal amounts of vitality and alertness will lead to clashes. There
is nothing wrong with this. Conflict is a natural sign of life, and it is
unhelpful to pretend that it does not exist.

Conflict takes two, two people or two sides, who perceive that
they are in disagreement. It is generated not only by personality
differences and opposing needs, it can also be created by the way
that organizations are structured.

Conflict can be handled effectively so that it is healthy and
productive. If it is properly managed, conflict can be an opportunity
for creativity and fresh approaches to problem-solving. The very
differences between people that cause clashes in the first place, such
as their various levels of knowledge and experience and their
differing beliefs, values and attitudes, can spark off new ideas. If
conflict is mismanaged or ignored, however, these differences can
lead to anger and frustration. Minor difficulties become huge
obstacles, and issues which are half dealt with or buried surface in
more destructive ways, often when they are least expected. The
greater the differences are between people, the more demanding is
the task to manage the conflict and prevent unhealthy anger. If you
suppress conflict, it will remain hidden, will not be resolved, and it
will emerge at some point in the future, probably in a more
destructive form.

It is helpful to recognize and anticipate likely sources of conflict.
This will help you to take steps to prevent disagreement becoming
heated anger, and will also enable you to diagnose the situation and
clarify critical issues. Once you have assessed likely sources of
disagreement you are in a good position to manage the conflict
effectively and achieve a positive outcome.

Sources of conflict

In Chapter 1 we looked at some of the needs which motivate us.
When clashes arises at work, it is often the result of conflicting
interests as we behave in ways that we think will get our needs met.

Three basic needs which govern our behaviour with other people at work are at the core of many interpersonal conflicts.

The need to be recognized

This is the desire to be seen as an individual, to be noticed and acknowledged. A person with very high needs in this area will behave to get attention and recognition. Recognition may be gained through positive or negative behaviour. People with low needs in this respect prefer not to stand out, and in some cases will do anything to avoid being the centre of attention.

The need for relationships

Some of us are motivated by our need to be liked. We like to have close relationships, and to give and receive affection. We value interpersonal relationships and make it a priority to develop friendships and a warm, supportive atmosphere. Others prefer to keep people more at arm's length. It is not important to us to 'bond' with our co-workers, and have close relationships with a selected few only.

The need for control

Some people are driven by a desire to be in charge, to influence what goes on. Their needs are met when they know that they are playing a leading role. This does not necessarily mean that they are seen to be in charge – their satisfaction can derive from their own knowledge that they have power and influence, and not from other people's awareness of this. Their need to be recognized is low. Others, however, may want to attain positions of power and prestige in order to satisfy their need for recognition. If you have low control needs, it means that you are not interested in taking the initiative and shaping what happens at work. You prefer not to make decisions or take the lead.

We are entirely dependent on other people for the satisfaction of our interpersonal needs. This means that we seek out people who will satisfy them, and avoid situations in which our particular needs will be thwarted. The advantage of this is that conflict can be anticipated. It is possible to predict situations and groups of people which are likely to be unsatisfying and unproductive, maybe because there are too many individuals with similar needs competing to get them met, or because their differences are too great to allow them to work together harmoniously.

ACTIVITY 44: Clashing needs

Think of a work disagreement in which you have recently been involved, or one which you have observed. How did each person behave? Which interpersonal need did each have?

Situation _____

	Behaviour	*Need*
Person a		

	Behaviour	*Need*
Person b		

Organizational sources of conflict

Resources

This covers everything that we must share with others. Resources may be financial, human or technical. When people are in competition for their share of a particular resource, feelings can run high as each strives to protect his or her own interests.

Roles

Lack of clarity or disagreement about roles and responsibilities is at the core of much conflict at work. You may experience clashes when there are conflicting expectations about your role or about other people's. This can lead to contradictory instructions being issued and misunderstandings about procedures and outcomes.

Goals

Conflict can arise when individuals' goals seem incompatible. Tension is generated when one party can achieve its entire aim only at the expense of the other party. The aims in question may cover a range of areas: money, position, influence, power, control.

Inaccurate or incomplete information

Conflict can be caused by issues to do with information. If not everyone has access to the same information, or if data is interpreted differently for and by different people and groups, hostility may well develop. When accurate and complete information is available to all the interested parties, there is greater trust and understanding and less chance of destructive conflict.

Your conflict management style

You will have developed your own approach to situations of conflict. Being aware of the strategies you instinctively use and assessing their effectiveness is the first step to managing conflict and disagreements at work. You can learn to handle conflict in a fair and effective way that keeps you calm and in control, and helps others to manage difficult situations without losing their cool.

ACTIVITY 45: How you manage conflict

This quiz will help you to find out your personal style of managing conflict.

1 You tell one of your team that the budget is spent and there is no more money for further purchases. The team member approaches another manager, who goes over your head and endorses the expenditure. What do you do?
   (a) Nothing. It is better not to make waves.
   (b) Say 'Over my dead body' and insist that the order is cancelled.
   (c) You smile and say, 'That's fine. I may have got my figures wrong.'
   (d) You arrange a time to discuss the matter with the other manager. You want to find out the background to his or her decision, and to reach an agreement about consistency.
   (e) You decide to discuss the matter of the finance with the other manager, but not to bring up the fact that your decision was countermanded.
2 Two of the people you work with are niggling each other with inflammatory comments, and you feel that a huge row is brewing. Do you:
   (a) Decide to keep out of the way until it blows over?
   (b) Tell them that you've noticed what is going on and insist that they stop this behaviour immediately?
   (c) Ask them not to upset everyone by creating such an unpleasant atmosphere?
   (d) Meet both parties to find a way of resolving the conflict between them?
   (e) Say, 'At least keep your voices down'?
3 Which two of the following statements most closely describe your attitudes? Tick the two descriptions that you choose.

TURNING CONFLICT INTO CO-OPERATION

	Tick	Score
(a) I put off dealing with conflict – it usually resolves itself.	☐	A
(b) I try to get the other person to see things my way.	☐	B
(c) I give in rather than try to change someone's opinion.	☐	C
(d) I disagree openly, then encourage discussion about our differences.	☐	D
(e) I agree to a middle ground rather than explore our differences.	☐	E
(f) Our team is great – we all get on really well.	☐	A
(g) I would rather make an enemy than lose an argument.	☐	B
(h) I focus on the non-controversial aspects of an issue.	☐	C
(i) I make sure that my ideas are heard and that others' ideas are heard.	☐	D
(j) I have a reputation for meeting people halfway.	☐	E

How to score: add up your numbers of A, B, C, D, E. Although most of us will use a variety of behaviours and may use different styles in different situations, your answers give an indication of your preferred approach. If your answers are mostly A, your style is Avoiding. If your answers are mostly B, your style is Competing. If your answers are mostly C, your style is Accommodating. If your answers are mostly D, your style is Collaborating, and if your answers are mostly E, your style is Compromising.

Avoiding

This means that you would prefer that a problem does not exist, so you refuse to acknowledge its existence. You have as little as possible to do with people who are in disagreement, and you avoid conflict by a variety of means. If a meeting is going to expose disagreements, you choose not to attend. You might say and even believe that you forgot, or had double-booked. If you go to the meeting, you may fall asleep. If you are in conflict with a particular person, you walk miles out of your way to avoid a face-to-face encounter. The ultimate avoidance strategy might be to quit your job rather than deal with the matter of conflict.

Competing

You have a confrontational approach based on a desire to win and get your way. This approach is based on power, and can rely on sometimes crude use of authority. Other strategies include citing the rule book and referring to policy. This approach focuses on finding solutions in which there are clear winners and losers, and little or no exploration of goals or values. A short-term view of conflict is preferred, with no planning for conflict resolution.

Accommodating

You prefer to believe that everything is fine. You want harmony, and put other people's needs before your own, apologizing and making concessions. You might change the subject if the discussion moves towards contentious issues, and you back away from disagreements. Confrontations and arguments upset you, so you give in easily in order to keep the peace.

Collaborating

Yours is a problem-solving approach, based on the principle that conflict can be managed so that nobody loses completely. This approach does not focus on right or wrong, or who is to blame, but sees defining the problem and seeking a solution as a joint activity. Sometimes solutions emerge that neither side would have come up with independently. Your style is both analytical and flexible. You listen to others' point of view, and want to work to find a solution that is as good as it can be.

Compromising

This is the middle ground. You will settle for a solution that is not satisfactory but at least is not destructive. No-one wins entirely and no-one loses entirely. This approach is reasonable and does involve negotiation and bargaining, but you can end up with the worst of all worlds.

Everyone's a winner

All the above approaches have advantages and disadvantages, costs and benefits. The first three styles discussed – avoiding, competing and accommodating – are likely to be the least effective if used consistently and exclusively. Strategies that see conflict as a fight which someone must win and someone must lose are not effective in the long run. They can create a cycle of aggression and defence which ultimately brings more tension and hostility. Those who perceive themselves as losers are likely to feel resentful, and their anger may emerge in destructive ways.

Compromising is a better alternative, although not ideal. It is essentially a lose-lose solution, in which no-one is entirely happy with what they have got, but can draw some satisfaction from the fact that at least the other side isn't happy either.

The approach that is likely to be most effective is collaborating. This is because collaboration is based on the principle of considering everyone's concerns, going beyond the positions that they have taken and looking at their needs and interests, then bringing all parties involved to the conclusion that everyone has won. It is not always possible to adopt this approach – there may not be enough time to explore needs and find common ground, or there may be too many people involved – but co-operating or collaborating in problem-solving is the most productive way to handle conflict. The collaborative approach works towards a win-win situation, in which all those involved feel as if they have gained something in the process. They may not literally win exactly what they had set out to gain, but in the course of examination and discussion they will have found different ways to meet their interests, and the sense of partnership that is created will make it far less likely that anger and hostility will emerge in the future.

Creative conflict

Conflict that is effectively managed in the way we have described can be constructive and creative. Factors which contribute to healthy conflict are:

(a) the people involved want to find a solution;
(b) different points of view are taken into account;
(c) arguments focus on issues rather than personalities.

Indications that conflict has been constructive are:

(a) better quality of communication between you and the other person;
(b) greater trust between you and the other person;

(c) both of you are satisfied with the outcome;

(d) you both have a greater ability to resolve future conflicts.

How to manage a conflict

There are four steps to managing a conflict.

Step one: acknowledge that conflict exists

Open it up

This step might mean that you take the initiative and speak to the person or people concerned: 'I think we have an issue that we should discuss.' It might mean that you respond to another's indication that something is wrong, such as your observation of growing anger, or of someone's angry response to an event. Apply what you have learnt about dealing with angry people, and choose the right time to broach the subject and to prepare the way for discussion. Establish the tone of the planned discussion by showing that the other party has something to gain by resolving the conflict, and make it clear that the discussion will be about the issues over which you are in conflict.

Set the scene

Think about the place you choose for your meeting. It might be a good idea to go for neutral territory so that neither side feels that it has a territorial advantage. Privacy is essential. If there really is no area in your workplace where you will be uninterrupted by phone calls and visitors, you may choose to go outside. Discussion will be most productive in an environment which is comfortable but not over-relaxed, so think about the kind of seating and seating arrangement you want. Do not sit face-to-face across a table – this position can seem confrontational and may trigger angry feelings associated with past experiences.

Make sure that the time is mutually convenient. Choose a time of day when you will not be distracted by mental or physical concerns. If you are hungry, or if your mind is on an urgent task, you may find it difficult to give your full attention to the discussion.

It is important to establish an atmosphere of mutual respect. You might consider setting some ground rules for your discussion, about confidentiality, for example. A time limit may be appropriate.

Step two: talk it through

Get more information

Both parties need to understand the other's position. Use 'I' statements to own your own feelings and to acknowledge your situation. Move the discussion on to look at interests rather than positions. Rather than getting stuck in an 'I want this and you want that' approach, look at what you will gain by achieving your respective goals. Ask questions such as 'How would gaining this affect you? How would work be better if you got what you are asking for?' This approach helps you to understand what is valuable to the other person and what is valuable to you, and so paves the way for finding a win-win solution. You are getting to the heart of the issue and discovering your real motivation, which may well have been unclear up to now.

Pay attention to verbal and non-verbal communication

Choose language which encourages a spirit of openness and co-operation. Phrases such as 'Suppose we . . .', 'What would happen if . . . ?', 'How would you feel if . . . ?' show a willingness to listen and explore ideas. You are moving from 'me against you' to 'us against the problem'.

Use reflective listening and responding to find out the other person's feelings and thoughts. Do not interrupt while the other person is speaking, and do not rush in with evaluations and judgements. If either party becomes angry, you may need to take a break or use other calming techniques until it is possible to resume the discussion.

Be attentive to non-verbal communication. Use your voice and your body language to encourage open discussion.

Agree on what the problem is

Continue to focus on issues and interests. Separate the problem from the person. You should now be in a position to define the essence of the problem and to agree the criteria for a successful outcome.

Step three: find solutions

Identify common ground

There will be some areas on which you can agree. Identify your shared concerns and focus on attitudes and needs you have in common. You should now have moved away from what divided you in the first place, although there may be points in the discussion at which you need to steer the debate back on to the right track.

Generate ideas

Come up with as many alternative courses of action as you can. You could brainstorm solutions, then evaluate each suggestion in terms of how far it will meet the needs of each party. Questions such as 'Which one of these options would be best for you?' are helpful at this stage.

Step four: agree on further action

Be ready to give to the other side what is more valuable to it than to you, and take in return what is more valuable to you than to the other. Make sure that your final agreement is specific and unambiguous. It is a good idea to describe the outcome on which you have agreed in terms of behaviour that can be observed and checked.

It might be that no action is needed – the process of talking the issue through may have revealed that the actual item of discussion was not as important as improving understanding and communication. Following a plan such as the one described does not necessarily mean that the problem gets solved. However, everyone has had an opportunity to express anger and hostility in a constructive, managed way. Anger at work is often linked to issues such as trust and perceptions of self-worth. This approach to conflict develops a climate of mutual respect and co-operation, making it easier to resolve difficulties and manage angry situations in the future.

Some blocks to effective conflict resolution

Resolving conflict effectively is a skill. It requires preparation and practice. A step towards becoming a skilful manager of conflict is identifying aspects of your attitudes and your behaviour that you might wish to change and develop. You can change your behaviour and you can acquire the skills to enable you to engage in creative conflict and channel anger and hostility into constructive discussion.

ACTIVITY 46: Attitudes to conflict

Decide how strongly you agree with each of the following statements. Give each statement a mark out of 10 to indicate how closely it describes your attitude.

1 I'm so committed to my ideas that   1 2 3 4 5 6 7 8 9 10
   I don't know when to give in.

2 I don't like to say that I have   1 2 3 4 5 6 7 8 9 10
   changed my mind.

3 I am not used to drawing out the   1 2 3 4 5 6 7 8 9 10
   opinions of others.

4 I don't like to admit that I am   1 2 3 4 5 6 7 8 9 10
   wrong

5 I don't like to interrupt other   1 2 3 4 5 6 7 8 9 10
   people if they are monopolizing
   time or attention.

6 I let others override my views.   1 2 3 4 5 6 7 8 9 10

7 I'd rather go along with the team   1 2 3 4 5 6 7 8 9 10
   than be seen to be in opposition.

8 I like to be personally involved   1 2 3 4 5 6 7 8 9 10
   even if it is not necessary.

9 I like to take charge even when   1 2 3 4 5 6 7 8 9 10
   it is not my responsibility.

10 I avoid discussions that are   1 2 3 4 5 6 7 8 9 10
   likely to become emotional.

11 I keep my feelings to myself   1 2 3 4 5 6 7 8 9 10
   even when others share.

12 I prefer logical discussion to   1 2 3 4 5 6 7 8 9 10
   personal persuasion.

Questions 1–4 focus on the kind of rigid behaviour that might prevent you from managing conflict effectively. You may cling too tenaciously to your own views, and/or neglect to encourage others to contribute. Questions 5–7 highlight the matter of confidence. It could be that in discussion and negotiation you yield your position too quickly, before the merits of your ideas have been properly considered. The question of intrusiveness is touched on in Questions 8–9. Possibly you become involved beyond the point where it is helpful. Perhaps you could use time more efficiently by taking a less involved role and allowing others more scope in exploring alternatives and looking for solutions. Questions 10–12 ask you to consider the impression you give. It could be that you seem aloof and unconcerned.

Skills

Conflict management requires the same kinds of communication skills that are necessary for all areas of managing anger. The stronger your skills at building and maintaining good relationships at work the greater will be your ability to handle conflict.

Activity 47: Communication skills

(a) How skilled are you in the following aspects of communication? Tick the appropriate column.

How good am I at:

	Good	So-so	Not good
showing that I acknowledge others' contributions?	☐	☐	☐
acknowledging differences of opinion between myself and others?	☐	☐	☐
choosing the right time to confront issues?	☐	☐	☐
responding appropriately to others' expressions of feelings?	☐	☐	☐
listening to others' points of view?	☐	☐	☐
using questions effectively?	☐	☐	☐
responding effectively?	☐	☐	☐
avoiding emotive words?	☐	☐	☐
using appropriate body language?	☐	☐	☐
defining problems clearly?	☐	☐	☐
finding common ground?	☐	☐	☐

(b) Choose three areas that you would like to develop. For each one, write down three things you can do to improve your skill.

Area to be developed   *Steps to take*

1 _____   (a) _____

                                             (b) _____

                                             (c) _____

2 _____   (a) _____

                                             (b) _____

                                             (c) _____

3 _____   (a) _____

                                             (b) _____

                                             (c) _____

When it's over

Conflicts are not always resolved satisfactorily. If you are unhappy with the outcome, do not allow feelings of anger, disappointment or resentment to get hold of you. Use positive self-talk to affirm that you did your best. Work out a statement along the lines of: 'Forget about it now. You did what you could. You did not become angry or irrational. Let it go.'

If a satisfactory conclusion was reached, affirm your success. 'I did well there. I controlled my feelings and listened to what was said. It was a good outcome.'

7

Putting it Right

Healing relationships damaged by anger

After an angry outburst

If you have exploded in anger with someone, or been at the receiving end of someone else's anger, you are left feeling uncomfortable. You may feel drained, exhausted, depressed or angry with yourself. The first thing that you should do is to acknowledge your feelings. Use a calming strategy to become less aroused, and use positive self-talk to encourage yourself to deal constructively with the aftermath of the event. You know that harbouring resentment, plotting revenge, withdrawing from the person or planning counter-attacks will be destructive. Your goal now is to make yourself feel calm and in control, and to establish or re-establish a working relationship with the other person.

The power of an apology

If you feel that you have been ill-tempered, snappy or outright angry with someone, and that your behaviour was wrong, then you should apologize for the way you acted. This should help to put things right for the other person, and will also help you to put the angry behaviour behind you.

Give some thought to how you offer your apology. You may choose to apologize in person, or on the phone, or in writing or email. Your decision will depend on the degree of anger shown, the circumstances and your relationship to the person involved. If you are apologizing for a brief spurt of anger or bad temper, a few words should be enough. If you are putting right a situation which is more serious or long-standing, you should go a little further than that. A face-to-face apology might seem difficult, but might be the most appropriate and generous way of expressing regret. Whether you are apologizing in person or on the phone, it is a good idea to plan what you are going to say (you will find this particularly helpful should you get the person's voice mail and wish to leave a message). When you apologize, refer to the incident without going into detail, and do not give excuses or reasons for your behaviour. This is not in order to make light of or gloss over what has happened, but to ensure that you do not get side-tracked from the act of apology or drawn into lengthy explanations which may seem self-justifying, and may detract from the impact of what you are saying. Make sure that the words 'sorry' or 'apologize' are heard.

Rebuilding a relationship

If a relationship at work suffers serious damage because of angry responses, you will probably wish to follow up your apology by making up for what you have done and showing willingness to prevent the situation arising again. Arrange a meeting in which you can discuss the incident or incidents in a calm and constructive way, without reopening the old wounds. Prepare yourself by relaxing your body and using calming self-talk, and remember to use 'I' statements to reveal and take responsibility for your feelings and wishes. It is a good idea to prepare beforehand what you want to say.

Forgiving and letting go

It can be very difficult to let go of our anger completely. If someone has done us a great wrong, with lasting significant effect, it is difficult not to think about it and to relive it. An event that happened years ago can seem fresher and more immediate every time you bring it to mind. The trouble is that nothing can change the circumstances or alter what has happened, and your anger is rekindled time and time again. You need to let go of the anger. The person who wronged you is not affected by your anger – those who suffer are yourself and the people in your life.

> Holding on to anger is like grasping a hot coal with the intent of throwing it at someone else; you are the one who gets burned.
>
> *Buddha*

Some wrongs are so enormous that the journey to forgiveness, should you choose to undertake it, would be lengthy and difficult, and you may well need expert support to help you to deal with the pain and anger. But for the kinds of workplace events that we have been discussing, the everyday situations that trigger our anger and that, for the sake of our mental and physical health, we need to control before they control us, forgiving and letting go is the final part of the process.

When you forgive someone who has wronged you, you release your anger and enable yourself to move on, leaving hostility and resentment behind you. Forgiveness is a choice. No-one can force you to forgive someone having wronged you, but if you decide to do so, you will feel calmer and more peaceful as a result. Religious leaders and psychologists focus on the emotional and spiritual benefits of forgiveness, and as you know, your physical health improves when you stop being eaten up by anger.

Forgive us our trespasses as we forgive those who trespass against us.

Jesus Christ

When you forgive someone, it does not necessarily mean that you forget what happened. You may in fact want to remember the situation and learn from it. You do, however, forgive the person for the specific wrong that was committed, and then put it behind you. You have cleared the account, nothing is owed, and there is a clean slate for the future.

Scene 19: Jammed photocopier

Reading her newspaper on the way to work, Yasmin sees some information that will add a lot of weight to the proposal that she will be making in the meeting first thing. In fact, she thinks, the figures in the article should just about clinch her argument. When she arrives, Yasmin heads straight for the photocopier, only to find it jammed. Hurriedly she pulls out the tray to clear the blockage, but has no success.

'Why do people do this!' she expostulates. 'Someone has jammed the machine, and just walked away and left it!'

Yasmin is thrown off her stride, and in the meeting does not present her case very well. She finds out that it was Hayley who had left the photocopier so that no-one could use it. Yasmin feels really angry with Hayley, and even some time after the incident finds that she is nursing a bit of a grudge against her. This makes Yasmin feel tense and uncomfortable.

Yasmin decides to forgive and let go. The incident is over; her feelings of annoyance are not going to change anything or make anything better. However, she can make things better for herself by letting go of uncomfortable and negative feelings and moving on. Yasmin chooses to forgive Hayley for her thoughtlessness, and in doing so gets rid of her anger.

ACTIVITY 48: Choosing to forgive

Practise forgiving and letting go. Recognize that although your anger and resentment may be justified, it will not alter what has happened and will only do you harm in the long run. Make a conscious decision to forgive and to let it go. Choose three situations in ascending order of importance or difficulty where it would be good for you to forgive a transgression. For each one, work out a statement that enables you to forgive and move on.

Incident   *Statement of forgiveness (to yourself)*

1 _____

2 _____

3 _____

Forgive yourself

Sometimes we find it hardest to forgive ourselves. We become angry with ourselves for a range of reasons – we fail to live up to our own standards, we wish we had handled events differently, we made a serious mistake. Self-anger is destructive and self-defeating. Rather than blame yourself when things go wrong, channel your energy into the following strategies for managing self-anger and learning to give yourself acceptance and forgiveness.

Set goals

Instead of suffering the pain of self-doubt and self-blame, decide what action you can take to help you put the situation right and move on. If you have made a mistake, do what you can to put it right and prevent it from happening again. If you regret something you said, do what you can to put it right, and focus on acquiring the skills to help you communicate more appropriately.

ACTIVITY 49: Set specific targets

Identify the situations in which you feel annoyed with yourself. You might blame yourself for finding it difficult to learn a new program or system, or for keeping quiet about something when you really wanted to speak out. For each situation, set a realistic, attainable goal. Your goals may be short-term or long-term.

When I am angry with myself   *What I can do about it*

e.g. Making mistakes and being   Learn to ask for help
slow   Go on a training course

1 _____

2 _____

3 _____

By deciding to do something about the situations which give rise to self-anger, you are putting your energy to constructive, productive use, and cutting short the cycle of angry thoughts and feelings.

Increase your self-esteem

Building a sense of your own worth is part of the process of understanding, accepting and forgiving yourself. If you have a sound degree of self-esteem, you have the confidence to solve problems and deal constructively with the challenges that face you. There are some ways of building your self-confidence and your ability to acknowledge your mistakes and let them go.

Get into the habit of giving yourself affirmations – positive statements about yourself. It is important that these statements are expressed in the positive as opposed to the negative. In other words, they affirm what you are and what you will do, not what you are not and what you won't do. Make them short and memorable, so that you can bring them to mind and repeat them easily. The kind of affirmation that you might use is: 'It's all right if I make mistakes' or 'I can choose to change my life.' You could identify some of your strong points and celebrate them in a statement such as: 'I have good friends' or 'I am very good at my job.' You can strengthen your belief in such statements by bringing to mind examples and illustrations of your positive qualities.

ACTIVITY 50: Affirmations

The most powerful affirmations are the ones you make up yourself. Compose three statements that you can use to affirm your self-worth.

1 _____

2 _____

3 _____

Forgiveness through understanding

When you get angry with yourself because of something you have done or said, or because of something you have failed to do or say, stand back and examine your behaviour. Ask yourself why you behaved in that way. What need were you seeking to meet with the particular behaviour? It could be that you behaved badly because of your need for control, or to be noticed. What influenced your actions? Certain beliefs or ideas may have been shaping your behaviour. What was the threat? What loss did you fear? When you are clear about your motivation, move on to acknowledge that you feel bad for what you did, but you know that your behaviour showed that you were trying to get particular needs met. Accept that you behaved as you did for certain reasons. Accept that you were doing what seemed best at the time with the knowledge that you had at the time. You do not have to approve of what you did to be able to forgive yourself.

How to become less angry

Managing your thoughts, feelings and behaviour so that you become less angry and become angry less frequently means making changes in the way that you think and in the way that you behave. The more tolerant and flexible you are, the less likely you are to fly off the handle. If you are physically calm and relaxed, you are less likely to respond to anger triggers than if you are tense and wound up.

Become more tolerant

As you know, we often respond with anger and impatience when people do not behave as we would like them to. Being tolerant does not mean putting up with unacceptable behaviour or adopting a *laissez-faire* attitude in which anything goes. What it does mean is allowing the other person to be different from you. You are accepting the difference, not judging it, not approving, not disapproving. Once you accept the difference, you are more able to see the situation from the other's perspective. This does not necessarily mean that you will be in agreement, but you will be more able to respond rationally and tolerantly to the behaviour of people whose background and view of the world is different from yours.

ACTIVITY 51: Your tolerance levels

(a) Check out your own prejudices. Pair up the descriptions in Column A with the people in Column B. Give your instinctive reaction.

Column A	*Column B*
Self-righteous	Female manager
Authoritative	A heterosexual co-worker
Stuck in the mud	Male manager
Unreliable	A happily married co-worker
Flighty	Someone who talks differently from you
Arrogant	Someone a generation older
Smug	A man having an office affair
Lazy	A homosexual co-worker
Upstart	A religious co-worker
Poor communicator	A woman having an office affair
Bossy	Someone from a different race or culture
Marriage-wrecker	Someone a generation younger
Sloppy	Someone with face piercings

PUTTING IT RIGHT

(b) Now try a random pairing of the words in each column. Notice any pairings that surprise you. Work out a statement you can use that will help you to increase your tolerance level and see people as individuals whose differences are assets to be valued.

Statement: _____

(c) Think of someone at work (a person about whom you have neutral or negative feelings) who is different from you in terms of culture, race, age, sexual orientation or level of education. Find three things to admire in this person's work performance. If possible, tell the person about one of the aspects that you have noticed.

Person	*Qualities*	*What I could say*
1		
2		
3		

You could take further steps to increase your tolerance and understanding of others, such as socializing with people of a generation older or younger than yourself, or having a discussion with someone who holds different political or religious views. The more you understand and accept the contexts in which other people live, the less likely you are to respond to problems and difficulties with irritation and annoyance, and the more likely you are to generate solutions and understanding.

Become more flexible

We saw earlier that rigid beliefs and ideas are often at the root of anger. It is very easy to slip into or adopt habits of thought and behaviour which, without our realizing it, become ingrained and limit our capacity for tolerance. However, rituals and habits can also be soothing and supportive. Try to strike a balance by maintaining and valuing the rituals which have a grounding, calming effect, and developing a more flexible approach with regards to habits which have become important to you without contributing significantly to your well-being.

ACTIVITY 52: Habits and rituals

(a) Make a list of your habits and rituals, at work and outside work. These are the routines that are important to you and which you would consider that you always or regularly engage in. They might include having your breaks at certain times, what you eat at particular mealtimes, the order in which you approach a task at work, reading a story to the children, having a drink after work, etc.

(b) For each example, decide to what extent the habit or ritual has a positive effect. Ask yourself:

What would I feel like if I stopped doing this?
What would I feel like if I changed this routine or part of it?
What do I gain by continuing with this particular behaviour?

For each routine, decide if you should continue with it (c), drop it (d), or modify it (m). Write in the appropriate letter.

(c) For the habits that you will modify, jot down next to each one the change that you will make. It could be something like eating or drinking differently, or approaching a task in a slightly different way. There is no need to adopt the change for ever – or you might end up exchanging one ritual for another! – but building in little differences increases your resilience and flexibility, and prevents you from getting locked into rigid patterns of thought and behaviour.

	Ritual	*c/d/m*	*Change*
1			
2			
3			
4			
5			
6			
7			
8			

In addition to making these small changes, you could try to take on some totally new activities, such as visiting somewhere you would normally not consider, or experimenting with your choice of film or television programme. Avoid getting stuck in a rut. No matter how secure and comfortable it may be, it becomes less so when you find it difficult to manage your angry reactions because you cannot adapt your way of thinking and responding.

Slow down

Certain personality types are prone to angry flare-ups. They have high levels of hostility and aggression, and it takes very little provocation to trigger their anger.

Scene 20: Typical Type A

Duncan taps his foot impatiently while waiting for the lift, and gives the button a few sharp jabs. He decides to take the stairs anyway – he can't afford to hang about wasting time – and pushes past two people who are walking up slowly. At his desk he opens the file he is working on, at the same time dialling Nazaar's extension number.

'Have you got those figures I asked for?' Duncan barks. 'I need them right now.'

'Well, good morning to you too,' says Nazaar. 'As it happens, I'm just finishing the last batch. Don't worry, I'll let you have them as soon as they are ready.'

Duncan feels a surge of irritation at Nazaar's laid-back attitude. 'That will have to do, then.'

'We got held up a bit yesterday, in fact,' says Nazaar. 'What happened was . . .'

Duncan writes some notes on the file that he is reading, hardly listening to what Nazaar is saying. He realizes that he will not get this project finished on time without buying in some temporary cover for Jill's absence, and that he should have planned to do so earlier.

'Got to go,' he interrupts, and dashes off to see the person who deals with the agency.

She shakes her head and says, 'This is very short notice, you know.'

'But I need someone from tomorrow! Why is it so difficult to get anything done around here?'

Your behaviour may be similar to Duncan's in every way or in some ways. You will undoubtedly have come across a Duncan – he may be the driver who overtook you quite unnecessarily on your way to work this morning, or your work colleague who does everything at top speed and has a highly competitive attitude. Duncan shows what heart specialists Meyer Friedman and Ray Rosenman categorize as Type A behaviour. Type A individuals tend to be ambitious and combative. They are always in a hurry, doing several things at once, and often rushing into projects without the preliminary planning necessary to achieve their goals. They thrive on challenge and deadlines, and in their drive to gain results can be intolerant of what they perceive as others' failings or weaknesses.

People like this are almost permanently geared up for action. Their bodies surge with adrenalin, their hearts thump, their muscles are tense. This high degree of arousal means that their anger can be easily triggered. At the other end of the scale is the Type B personality, which is more tolerant, calm and easygoing, less likely to flare up or respond aggressively. The following exercise will help you to find out to which category you belong.

ACTIVITY 53: Your behaviour type

Read the following descriptions of behaviour. For each one, tick the column that indicates how far it applies to you.

Characteristic	Very true	Sometimes true	Not at all true
Very competitive	☐	☐	☐
Does everything quickly	☐	☐	☐
Intolerant of delays	☐	☐	☐
Unable to relax	☐	☐	☐
Does several things at the same time	☐	☐	☐
Ambitious	☐	☐	☐
Interrupts people	☐	☐	☐
Speaks emphatically and forcefully	☐	☐	☐
Physically tense	☐	☐	☐

Look at your number of ticks in the first two columns. These indicate areas in which you could change your behaviour in order to become less anger-prone. By adopting some Type B ways of behaving you will feel calmer and be more able to control your responses. Of course your drive and ambition to succeed is a positive quality, one that is valued in the work environment. But inappropriate anger can prevent you from performing effectively and achieving your goals. Channel some of your drive and determination into making the kind of change that will work to your advantage.

ACTIVITY 54: Changing behaviour

Choose three examples of your Type A behaviour that you could change. Specify the change that you will make.

Behaviour	*Change*
e.g. overtaking when driving	allow two cars to overtake me

1 _____

2 _____

3 _____

Learn to relax

You are already aware of the importance of physical relaxation when you are dealing with your own or someone else's anger. Relaxation is a great way to unwind and to generate feelings of calm and control. To get the utmost benefit from this gift to your mind and body, practise some of the following relaxation techniques. You will learn how to activate the part of your nervous system called the parasympathetic side. This system reverses the workings of the sympathetic side, the one that arouses you, by calming you down. If you are under constant pressure, it is likely that this system is under-used because it never gets a chance to come into operation.

Relaxation triggers biochemical changes in the body, as mood-altering chemicals are manufactured. In particular, the production of the neurotransmitter serotonin brings about feelings of happiness and calm.

Practise breathing properly

Correct breathing will make you feel calm. What you should aim for is breathing in a continuous cycle using your diaphragm to control the flow of breath. You should feel your stomach, not your chest, moving as you breathe. You should not pause before inhaling or exhaling; as you may have noticed, when you are feeling angry you tend to pause before inhaling.

Try this breathing exercise, which you can do anywhere. Sit comfortably in an upright position. It is important to sit up straight, because if you slouch your diaphragm cannot work properly, and you breathe in your chest area. Take a deep slow breath, counting to five as you do so. Your chest should rise as you breathe in. Hold your breath for a second, then breathe out slowly to a count of five. Breathe in again, and out again. Make every breath steady and even. You should feel your chest stay up, while your stomach gently rises and falls.

You can do this exercise for ten seconds, or for a few minutes. To reinforce the effect of your breathing, as you breathe out you could say a word such as 'calm', keeping it up until all the air is expelled from your lungs.

Unwind your body

You could use relaxation tapes or CDs or classes to teach you how to get rid of all the tension from your body. A simple technique, one that is particularly effective when used with the breathing exercise described above, is to concentrate on each part of your body in turn, tensing and relaxing each set of muscles systematically. Begin with your head and face, move on to your neck and jaw, then down to each arm and leg. Concentrate on feeling the tension in the muscles as you clench them, and the feeling of release as you breathe out and let the tension flow away.

Something else you might like to try is relaxing each set of muscle groups, starting with your toes and working up, accompanying the movements with self-instructional talk. Begin by breathing deeply and rhythmically. As you concentrate on your toes, say something like, 'I am so calm and relaxed. I am breathing smoothly and deeply, and becoming more and more relaxed. My toes are becoming heavy ... the tension is draining away ...' Make up your own script for this exercise. Once you become used to doing it, just beginning the technique will make you relaxed.

Do these exercises, or part of them, when you feel yourself getting worked up, and do them as a regular part of your anger management programme. You will become calmer and less likely to respond angrily to provocations.

Meditation

Meditation is a technique which has been used for over 2,500 years. It brings you into a calmer state of being by emptying thoughts and preoccupations from your conscious mind. The idea is to bring peace to your mind by entering into a state of stillness in which your attention is focused on your state of being, not on thoughts. You move away from yourself by concentrating on an object or image, such as a flower or a beautiful stone or shell, or even your breathing, which will help to generate a feeling of peace and tranquillity. In Transcendental Meditation you focus on a mantra, a word or a phrase such as the Sanskrit syllable 'Om' which is chanted inwardly or out loud.

There are various forms of meditation – what works for one person may not work for someone else, and it may be that this kind of technique is just not for you. You do need to practise every day if you are to attain lasting benefits, and it is best to meditate daily at the same time, in the same place, which should be tranquil and comfortable.

Try a simple exercise. Find an appropriate place where you will not be disturbed for 20 minutes or so. Get into a comfortable position in which your back is straight, and first of all concentrate on breathing and relaxing. Become mindful of your whole body. Listen to your breathing and the beat of your heart. Focus on your chosen image. When other thoughts intrude, notice that your attention has wandered, and bring it back to the image. Do this for a few minutes at first, then build up the time you spend, until you feel your mind becoming calm.

Visualization

You can use visualization to help you to manage your emotional state. There are two ways you could use this powerful tool: to strengthen your ability to cope with particular situations, and to help you to unwind and achieve a state of calm well-being.

As a method of relaxation, creative imaging, or visualization, uses specific techniques to counteract negative states of mind, such as tension, anger, anxiety. It is similar to meditation in that you use images associated with peace and calm in order to bring your mind down from its state of arousal, and, like meditation, this may not be a technique for you. As with the relaxation exercises discussed earlier, when you get used to these activities, your mind responds very quickly to what it associates with calm, and so you can bring yourself to a peaceful state more and more easily. The relaxation response can become more easily activated than the anger response.

Visions of calm Choose a scene that you associate with peace and harmony. For many people, the thought of lying on a warm, sunny beach induces a feeling of calm and well-being. For others, it could be a walk in the country or through a wood. It is best to create your own scene, with images that work for you. You know which picture will give you most pleasure and make you most relaxed. The following example gives you an idea of the kind of script you could use – there are thousands to choose from.

Go somewhere quiet where you will not be disturbed. Relax and close your eyes. Concentrate on breathing deeply and rhythmically. Imagine that you are ... lying in a flowery meadow. The grass is thick and springy underneath your back. The scent of the flowers fills your nostrils. A gentle breeze touches your face. The sun is warm on your face and body. With every breath, the grass supports you ... lifts you up ... you are weightless ... the sun warms you through and through ... it enters every limb ... your limbs are so heavy ... they sink down ... tension melts away ... all your muscles loosen, dissolve ... your eyelids are heavy ... you are so relaxed ...

As you visualize the scene, say to yourself, 'I am so relaxed and warm ... I am so relaxed and warm ...' Gradually bring yourself out of the scene. Open your eyes and stretch.

Visions of coping Use visualization to help you to deal with angry situations. Your imagination and your senses can help you to prepare for difficult encounters.

Think of a situation in which you frequently become annoyed, and in which you would like to behave calmly. Close your eyes and imagine yourself in that situation.

Where are you?
Who else is there?
What is your body doing?
What are you thinking?
What are you feeling?

At this point, allow yourself to feel your angry response. Now think about how you want to behave. Relax. Take a deep breath and feel yourself breathing steadily and slowly. Imagine yourself responding as you would like to.

What do you say?
What does your voice sound like?
Where are you positioned?
What is your facial expression?

What are you doing with your hands?
What are you thinking?
What are you feeling?
How is the other person responding?

You can go through the scene several times until you can see and feel yourself managing your emotions successfully.

Anger-proofing your workplace

Behave assertively

Whatever your position at work, whether or not you are a manager or leader, the way you communicate can contribute to angry and frustrated feelings, or can contribute towards an atmosphere of calm and co-operation. Expressing yourself assertively in your verbal and non-verbal communication encourages others to adopt the same style of communication, and creates trust and mutual respect. In an environment in which people feel respected and are listened to, anger and hostility are likely to be managed effectively and prevented from getting out of control. If your behaviour shows that you respect people and value them as individuals you are helping to create a positive and productive working atmosphere.

Non-verbal messages

Your way of walking and standing, your facial expressions and the types of gestures you use give a message to other people about the kind of person you are. If your behaviour is perceived as aggressive, people may respond to you in similar mode, or they may act defensively. If your behaviour is seen to be weak and too eager to please, not only do you fail to inspire confidence in others, but you are just as likely to generate hostility and frustration. Avoid habits of behaviour which can make you feel tense and angry, and can cause negative emotions in others.

What to avoid	What to practise
staring	steady eye contact
not meeting people's eyes	composed facial expressions
frowning	frowning when you mean it
sneering	relaxed upright position
smiling when you don't mean it	smiling when you mean it

What to avoid	*What to practise*
looking bored	loose arms and legs
covering face with hands	relaxed hands
tightly folded arms	open palms
pointing finger	
hand thumping	
pacing up and down	
foot tapping	

What you say and how you say it

There are some words and expressions which are so often associated with blame and anger that you should try not to use them. At the same time, recognize that there is no point in using non-inflammatory language in a tone of voice that contradicts the words. If you hiss or shout the words, 'Of course I'm not angry', accompanied by one of the gestures from the 'avoid' list above, you are giving a mixed message which will have an unsettling and provocative effect.

What to avoid	*What to practise*
shouting	clear voice
speaking very quietly	level voice
mumbling	I think . . . what do you think?
whining or wheedling	I feel
mocking	Why don't we . . . ?
interrupting	What can we do about
You ought . . .	I will not accept this situation
You should . . .	
That's typical of you . . .	In my opinion . . .
The trouble with you is . . .	Let's . . .
Don't be angry with me, but . . .	
I'm not being horrible but . . .	

Anger-free communication

You can create a work environment in which anger or conflict is managed healthily and constructively. Apply the following guidelines:

communicate
listen
understand goals and objectives
give praise and recognition
look for solutions
take responsibility for your feelings
be fair and consistent
understand needs and motivation.

Create a calm environment

The conditions in which you work can have a calming effect, or they can contribute to tension. Although you may not be able to influence decisions about your working environment, as far as you are able you could apply some ideas about how to avoid high levels of arousal and to maintain a sense of inner peace and harmony.

Colour

If your workplace is painted bright red, it could be contributing to angry and aggressive feelings. Colour can affect our moods, and in some cases can affect us physically, although the effect will differ from person to person. Red is a stimulating colour, which is great in some circumstances, but may be too agitating for anyone whose anger is easily triggered. Red light can in fact cause blood pressure to rise, while blue light can have the opposite effect. Blues and greens are thought to be cool and soothing, while violet is thought to make us receptive to calmness and spirituality. No matter what shade the walls are, you may be able to introduce appropriate colours, with plants, for example, or your personal belongings. Looking at a colour that you associate with peace and harmony will remind you of the importance of controlling and managing hostile responses.

Light and air

Without natural light and adequate ventilation, you may become moody and edgy, and more prone to anger. Work near a window if you can, and go outside as much as possible, especially when it is sunny.

Take breaks

Have breaks during the working day. Use the time to relax and unwind, or get some fresh air. You could take the opportunity to practise one of the breathing exercises discussed earlier, and you could listen to some music. Music can have a very calming effect. Some types of music can lower your heart rate and act as a relaxant, and can even help your breathing. There are tapes and CDs of music specifically chosen for its relaxing effect, or you could make your own selection. Experiment to find what works for you. Look for something which is gentle, slow, repetitious.

Use anger to heal

Anger can be healing. If you express your anger appropriately, you can make a situation better straight away, before destructive emotions can take hold. Don't let anger, yours or anyone else's, rule or ruin your life. You are able to manage and take responsibility for the way you think, feel and behave.

Respect the power of anger. Accept it as a sign that something needs to be changed, and channel it constructively to improve your working life and relationships. Once you understand the nature and cause of anger, harness its power as a source of strength. The suggestions made in this book will help you to explore your emotional and behavioural responses, and to express your feelings in ways that do not damage you or anybody else, but rather help to build honest and productive communication. Repressing and denying anger has destructive effects, and prevents healing and growth. Managing anger in a responsible way – feeling it, expressing it and releasing it – makes it a constructive emotion and a powerful impetus for change. The changes that you are enabled to bring about will result in personal peace.

Further Reading

Dryden, Windy (1996) *Overcoming Anger*. London: Sheldon Press.

Lindenfield, Gael (2000) *Managing Anger*. London: Thorsons.

Luhn, Rebecca H. (1992) *Managing Anger*. London: Kogan Page.

Ruben, Theodore Isaac (1969) *The Angry Book*. Basingstoke: Collier Macmillan.

Williams, Redford and Williams, Virginia (1993) *Anger Kills*. London: HarperCollins.

Index

UNIVERSITY COLLEGE Library CORK